TREASURES *of the* EARTH

Treasures of the Earth

Rocks, Minerals, Crystals, and Gems

Senior art editor Emma Clayton
Senior editor Steven Carton
Senior US editor Megan Douglass
Managing editor Rachel Fox
Managing art editor Owen Peyton Jones
Production editor Joss Moore
Production controller Gillain Reid
Jacket designer Emma Clayton
Jacket editor Steven Carton
Designers Amy Child, Laura Gardner, Tory Gordon-Harris, Rhys Thomas
Illustrators Andrew Lyons, Jeff Langevin
Team lead, picture research Sumedha Chopra
Assistant picture researchers Geetam Biswas, Shubhdeep Kaur, Jo Walton
DTP designer Vijay Kandwal
Publisher Andrew Macintyre
Art director Mabel Chan

Authors Steven Carton, Ian Fitzgerald, Phil Hunt, Anthea Lacchia
Consultants Helen Molesworth, Cally Oldershaw

First American edition, 2025
Published in the United States by DK Publishing, a division of Penguin Random House LLC
1745 Broadway, 20th Floor, New York, NY 10019

Copyright © 2025 Dorling Kindersley Limited
25 26 27 28 29 10 9 8 7 6 5 4 3 2 1
001–349721–August/2025

All rights reserved.
Without limiting the rights under the copyright reserved above, no part of this publication may be reproduced, stored in or introduced into a retrieval system, or transmitted, in any form, or by any means (electronic, mechanical, photocopying, recording, or otherwise), without the prior written permission of the copyright owner.

No part of this publication may be used or reproduced in any manner for the purpose of training artificial intelligence technologies or systems.

Published in Great Britain by Dorling Kindersley Limited

ISBN: 978-0-5939-6948-9

Printed and bound in China

www.dk.com

This book was made with Forest Stewardship Council™ certified paper—one small step in DK's commitment to a sustainable future. Learn more at www.dk.com/uk/information/sustainability

Contents

6
What are treasures?

Treasures of the Earth	8
What is a mineral?	10
Properties of minerals	12
What is a gem?	14
From gemstone to jewel	16
What treasure means to us	18

20
Native elements

Gold	22
Golden place	26
Silver	28
Treasures of ancient Egypt	30
Copper	32
Diamond	34
Deathly diamonds	36

38
Gemstones

Sapphire	40
Ruby	42
Treasures of India	46
Spinel	48
Azurite and Turquoise	50
Malachite	52
Quartz	54
Crystal clear	58
Amethyst	60
Chalcedony	62
Treasures of ancient Greece and Rome	66
Agate	68
Unique structure	72
Jasper	74
Ancient stripes	78
Treasures of China	80
Opal	82
Moonstone and Sunstone	86
Labradorite	88
Lapis lazuli	90
Jade	92
Treasures of the Americas	96
Tourmaline	98
Emerald	102
Beryl	104
Garnet	106
Buried treasure	110
Zircon	112
Topaz	114
Treasures of West Africa	116

118
Other treasures

Pearl	120
Shell	124
Fossilized beauty	126
Mother-of-pearl	128
Tsimshian masks	130
Treasures of Oceania	132
Jet and Peanut wood	134
Amber	136
Eighth Wonder	138
Coral	140
Obsidian	142
Sandstone and Limestone	144
Colors and stripes	146
Marble	148
Mining marble	150
Treasures of Japan	152
Glossary	154
Index	156
Index / Acknowledgments	158
Acknowledgments	160

A note on abbreviations

Some dates in this book may include the abbreviation BYA, short for "billion years ago," or MYA, short for "million years ago." Other dates have BCE and CE after them. These are short for "before the Common Era" and "Common Era." The Common Era dates from when people think Jesus Christ was born. Where the exact date of an event is not known, "c." is used. This is short for the Latin word circa, meaning "around," and indicates that the date is approximate.

What are treasures?

Our fascination with beautiful materials stretches back thousands of years—but how are rocks, minerals, crystals, and gems formed, and what makes them valuable? How do we enhance these natural treasures, and how have we used them throughout history?

Treasures of the Earth

Our planet produces incredible things. All of the materials we use in our day-to-day lives come from Earth, as do the sparkling gemstones and precious metals that we value greatly. These treasures have been forming for millions, if not billions, of years before humans walked Earth. They are made from the rocks beneath our feet, the minerals that make up the rocks, and the elements that form those minerals.

Rock types

We organize rocks into three main groups: igneous, sedimentary, and metamorphic. Igneous rocks form when magma (molten rock) solidifies. Sedimentary rocks form from the compacted fragments of other rocks, and metamorphic rocks form when rocks are heated and pressurized.

Igneous basalt
Basalt is an extrusive igneous rock—it forms above ground. Intrusive igneous rocks form below ground.

Sedimentary shale
This shale is made up of layers of clay and mud that were squeezed tightly together over time, becoming sedimentary rock.

Metamorphic gneiss
Gneiss started out as igneous granite. The temperature and pressure deep underground squashed the granite's minerals into clear layers.

Tourmaline is a mineral that forms multicolored crystals.

Minerals
A mineral is a naturally occurring solid with a distinctive crystal structure and a specific chemical composition. There are many types of minerals, and some can be cut and polished to make jewelry.

Amphibole gneiss, a metamorphic rock

Rocks
Rocks are a combination of mineral particles, mixed up together. A gneiss like this one can contain a wide range of different minerals, including amphibole, feldspar, and quartz.

8 | WHAT ARE TREASURES?

The rock cycle

Earth's rocks and minerals don't remain in the same form forever. Over millions of years they move, form, melt, and transform, in a process known as the rock cycle. Much of this activity occurs around the edges of Earth's tectonic plates: enormous rocky chunks of Earth's surface that move around, slowly pushing into each other.

Igneous rocks
When magma (liquid rock) cools, it solidifies, becoming igneous rock. This can happen above or below Earth's surface.

Wind and weather slowly wear away at the rock on Earth's surface, breaking tiny pieces off.

Rivers and streams carry sand and mud toward the sea.

Layers of tiny pieces of sediment (such as mud and sand) build up underwater.

Sedimentary rocks
Over time, water compacts sediment so much that it becomes solid sedimentary rocks.

Rocks melt to form magma.

Tectonic plate movement

Metamorphic rocks
Rocks close to volcanoes or near where Earth's plates move get baked and squashed, becoming metamorphic.

Gold was one of the first metals ever used.

Gold is often found alongside quartz crystals.

Native elements
These chemical elements occur in nature in a pure form, not mixed with any other elements. They include metals such as gold, silver, and copper, as well as nonmetals such as diamonds and graphite (both are forms of carbon).

Rhodochrosite crystals form shapes with many sides.

Crystals
A crystal is a solid structure with its atoms arranged in a particular repeating three-dimensional pattern. Natural crystals are quite rare, because they need time and space to grow inside cavities and cracks.

Amber is fossilized tree resin, which is millions of years old.

Organic gems
Organic gems are made by animals or plants. They include fossilized tree resin (amber) or wood (jet), coral and shell from sea creatures, and pearls, which are produced by shellfish.

TREASURES OF THE EARTH | 9

What is a mineral?

Minerals are solid substances that have formed naturally on Earth. They are the ingredients that make up rock. There are more than 4,000 minerals on Earth and they tend to form crystals with defined shapes. Scientists sort them into groups according to their chemical and physical properties. Here are the main groups.

Celestine is a sulfate that takes its name from its celestial (sky) blue colors. It is used in fireworks.

Amblygonite is a rare mineral found in granites.

Sulfates
When metals combine with sulfur and oxygen, sulfate minerals are formed. Sulfates appear in rocks such as limestone.

Phosphates
Containing phosphorus and oxygen, phosphates typically have vivid colors—such as turquoise.

In its natural form, silver can appear as a mass of tendrils, as in this sample growing in quartz.

Striations, which look like long parallel lines, are common on pyrite cubes.

Pyrite is a sulfide that often forms cube-shaped crystals.

This rock combines blue azurite, a carbonate, with chrysocolla, a turquoise silicate mineral.

Native elements
While most minerals are made of a combination of chemical elements, native elements such as gold and silver are found in nature in a relatively pure form.

Sulfides
When the element sulfur is combined with a metal, a sulfide is formed. These minerals can be valuable sources of lead, copper, and zinc.

Carbonates
A combination of a carbon and oxygen with a metal, carbonates include malachite and calcite, the main ingredient in the sedimentary rock limestone.

Sapphire—the blue variety of the oxide corundum—is the most valuable blue gemstone.

Fluorite, a halide, forms perfect cube-shaped crystals. It is used in smelting and in glass production.

Olivine, a silicate mineral, is an important component of Earth's upper mantle.

Oxides
A combination of oxygen and metals, oxides range from gemstones, such as rubies and sapphires, to rust, which forms when iron reacts with oxygen and water.

Halides
This mineral group forms when metals combine with the elements fluorine, chlorine, bromine, and iodine. Halides include halite, the common salt used in cooking.

Silicates
Silicates are the most common of all minerals on Earth, with more than 1,000 different minerals sharing a basic structure: one silicon atom surrounded by four oxygen atoms.

WHAT IS A MINERAL? | 11

Properties of minerals

Each mineral has a unique range of properties that can help us identify it. They include how hard the mineral is, how it bends, and how it breaks. These same properties determine how useful minerals will be as gemstones: gems need to hold their shape and not be easily scratched or shattered.

Talc — Talc is soft, and easily scratched with just a fingernail.

Gypsum

Calcite

Fluorite

Apatite — A knife can scratch apatite, but barely.

Fingernail — Your fingernails have a Mohs hardness of around 2.5.

Copper coin — If a mineral can be scratched by a copper coin, its hardness is less than 3.5.

Knife — The blade of a knife measures between 5 and 6 on the Mohs scale.

Hardness

In minerals, hardness is defined by how easy a substance is to scratch. German mineralogist Friedrich Mohs developed a scale for measuring this in 1812. It uses 10 standard minerals arranged on a scale of hardness from 1 to 10, where 1 is the most easily scratched.

Fracture

If you hit a mineral with a hammer, it will eventually break. However, minerals don't all break in the same way. "Fracture" describes the way in which a mineral breaks—each type influences how the mineral appears in finished pieces.

Conchoidal fracture
When a mineral breaks into surfaces with a smooth, shell-like appearance, it is called conchoidal fracture.

Concentric lines
Obsidian

Even fracture
Minerals with even fracture break into surfaces that are generally flat, but have a rough texture.

Chalcopyrite

Hackly fracture
Minerals with hackly fracture break into uneven surfaces with jagged edges and sharp points.

Jagged edges
Gold

Cleavage

The word "cleavage" is used to describe how easily a mineral cleaves (breaks) along its layers. If a mineral breaks cleanly in straight lines, creating shiny, smooth surfaces, it is said to have perfect cleavage. Some minerals have no cleavage, or cleave less perfectly.

The surfaces of this calcite show perfect cleavage.

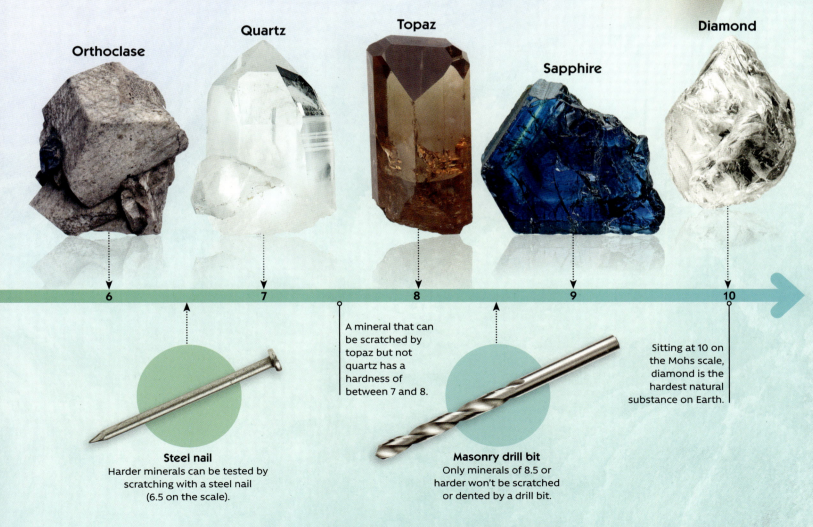

Orthoclase — 6
Quartz — 7
Topaz — 8
Sapphire — 9
Diamond — 10

Steel nail
Harder minerals can be tested by scratching with a steel nail (6.5 on the scale).

A mineral that can be scratched by topaz but not quartz has a hardness of between 7 and 8.

Masonry drill bit
Only minerals of 8.5 or harder won't be scratched or dented by a drill bit.

Sitting at 10 on the Mohs scale, diamond is the hardest natural substance on Earth.

PROPERTIES OF MINERALS | 13

What is a gem?

Gemstones are minerals (and sometimes organic material) that are considered valuable. What makes them valuable varies: it might be that they are rare, beautiful, or durable. Gemstones are usually cut and polished to create gems, which are used in jewelery. Most gemstones are made from crystals, which are solid materials with atoms arranged in a highly ordered, repeating pattern.

Playing with light

The way light interacts with gemstones is central to their beauty, color, and sparkle. Each gemstone bends, reflects, and transmits light in its own way.

Luster
The way light reflects off the surface of a gem is called luster. Different lusters have different levels of brilliance and shine and textures, such as waxy or greasy.

Refraction
Light bounces around inside a gem, changing direction and speed in an effect called refraction. This can result in "fire," flashes of colors seen as the gem moves.

The stem appears twice— known as double refraction.

Color
Some types of gemstone come in just one color, while others have a variety of color possibilities. Colors can also vary inside a single gem.

Idiochromatic gemstones come in just one color.

Particolored stones have more than one color in the same gem.

Allochromatic stones come in a range of colors.

Pleochroic stones seem to be different colors from different angles.

Durability
Being able to resist cracks and wear and tear is a desirable quality in a gem, as is having a long-lasting color. Diamonds are the hardest gemstones and have excellent durability.

Beauty
Everyone has their own idea of what is beautiful, but in gems beauty is usually linked to light and color play, such as the colorful patterns in black opal. It can also be linked to the style of a gemstone's cut.

Rarity
A gemstone's rarity is how unusual it is. It might be carved from a rare mineral, or discovered in a remote place. Particular colors can also be rare.

Creating gems

Most gems are made naturally by Earth, but some can be made in a laboratory. These synthetic gems are created by melting or dissolving mineral ingredients and coloring agents, then cooling them under controlled temperatures and pressure. They are very hard to tell apart from natural gems, but gem experts called gemologists have particular ways to identify them.

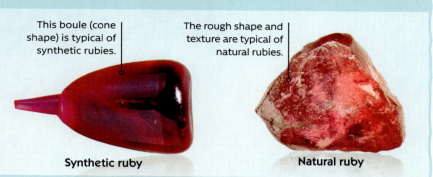

This boule (cone shape) is typical of synthetic rubies.

The rough shape and texture are typical of natural rubies.

Synthetic ruby

Natural ruby

Crystal shapes

A crystal's shape is based on its unit cell—the smallest repeating structure of atoms in the crystal. As the crystal grows, this pattern repeats in a regular way. The external shape a crystal forms is called its habit, which depends on the conditions in which it grew, such as temperature, pressure, and available space.

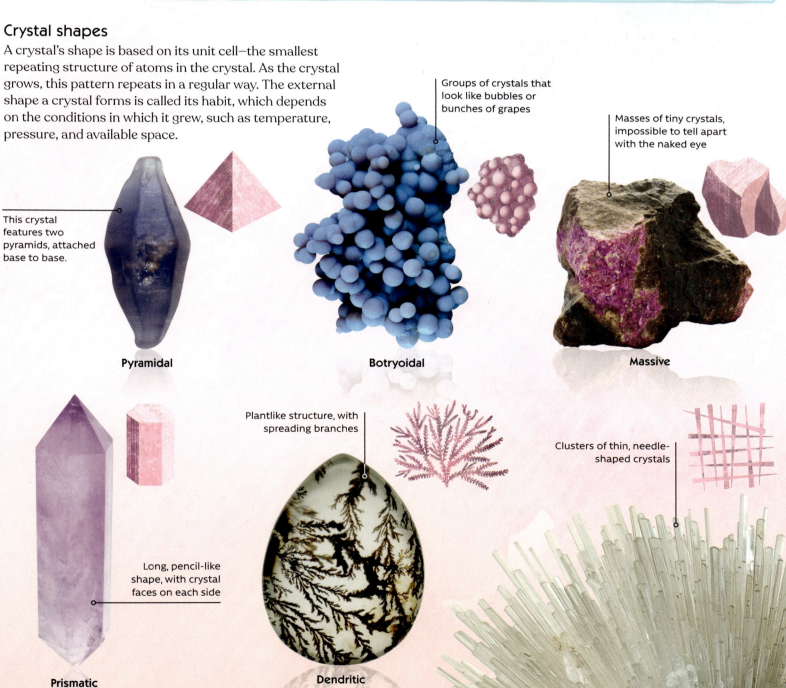

This crystal features two pyramids, attached base to base.

Groups of crystals that look like bubbles or bunches of grapes

Masses of tiny crystals, impossible to tell apart with the naked eye

Pyramidal

Botryoidal

Massive

Plantlike structure, with spreading branches

Clusters of thin, needle-shaped crystals

Long, pencil-like shape, with crystal faces on each side

Prismatic

Dendritic

Acicular

From gemstone to jewel

Gemstones undergo remarkable journeys before they become sparkling jewels. They begin buried deep inside Earth, where temperatures can reach 2,192°F (1,200°C). Once discovered, each stone is carefully polished and cut, to make it shine.

Crystal
Crystals naturally grow into defined shapes, controlled by their chemical makeup. These shapes often determine the way the gem is cut.

Cutting
The stone is cut, giving it flat surfaces called facets. The facets absorb and reflect light, making the stone sparkle.

Polishing
To improve how they reflect light, the crystals are sawed, ground, and polished into particular shapes.

Gemstone
Almost all gems begin as crystals embedded in a host rock known as the matrix. These rough gemstones must be taken from the rock.

Jewel
Finally, the gemstone is ready to be made into a finished piece. This might mean being combined with other stones and set in a precious metal.

Rough, cut, and polished
At first, gemstones look quite ordinary, like colorful rocks. To reveal their full beauty, they must be separated from the rock, cut into shape, before being polished.

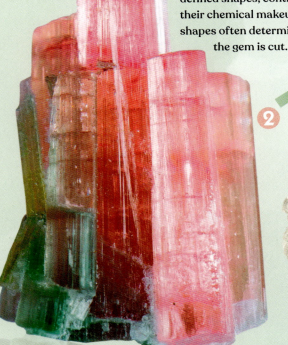

16 | WHAT ARE TREASURES?

Gem cuts

Gemstones can be cut in several different ways. These styles can highlight an individual stone's best features, or remove any imperfections. Cutting reduces a gemstone's weight, but if done well, it should increase the gem's value.

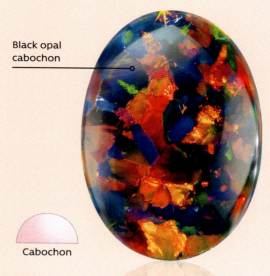

Brilliant cut
A brilliant cut uses many triangular or kite-shaped facets to reflect light inside the stone, making the gem really sparkle. This cut was first developed for diamonds.

Carving
Some gemstones can be carved. The two main styles are where the design rises up from the background (cameos), and where the design is cut into the surface (intaglios).

Cabochon
This is one of the oldest, simplest, and most popular cuts. It is smooth, with a domed top and often a flat back, and is usually used to show off colors and patterns inside stones.

Step cut
A step cut has long, flat, rectangular facets that look like steps. It is used to enhance a gemstone's color, at the expense of sparkle.

Mixed cut
A mixed cut combines the facets used in brilliant and step cuts, which helps show both the color and brilliance of a gemstone.

Fancy cuts
Gemstones that are cut to create unusual outlines are sometimes called "fancy." Fancy shapes include ovals, pears, and hearts.

The four Cs (and one R)

Gemstones are valued according to four "C's": carat, cut, clarity, and color. There is also one "R": rarity. All of these are taken into consideration when gemologists and jewelry dealers are assessing a gemstone.

Fancy, heart-shaped gemstone

Carat	Cut	Clarity	Color	Rarity
How heavy the stone is, usually measured in carats.	A skilled cut will make a gemstone more valuable.	The fewer fractures or inclusions, the better.	Vivid and intense colors are more highly valued.	Stones that are hard to find are more valuable.

FROM GEMSTONE TO JEWEL | 17

Religion
Precious metals and stones have long been a part of religious objects and ceremony. This 1,800-year-old Ecuadorian high priest's headdress is made of gold, which symbolized the sun god.

Holes enabled several shells to be strung together like a necklace.

This shell has been painted.

Dressing up
The desire to stand out by wearing stones and other forms of jewelery even predates our species. These shells were used as jewelery by Neanderthals, who lived around 300,000–100,000 years before the first modern humans.

The sun-god Inti was the bringer of light and energy to the world.

In China, Jade was believed to grant immortality.

Folk beliefs
Treasures have been linked with various beliefs since the dawn of civilization. This jade *cong* comes from ancient China and may have been used in ceremonial rituals.

What treasure means to us

For millennia, humans have assigned various layers of meaning to the stones, metals, and other materials found in the world around us.

Certain treasures have become associated with concepts such as good luck, health, and happiness, while others serve practical purposes, as with metal tools or gold currency. From decorative shells strung together by our prehistoric ancestors to the intricate craftsmanship of royal crowns, natural treasures have always been intertwined with the things that matter most to us.

Tools
Our human ancestors used stone to make the first tools around 3.3 MYA. More recently, gemstones have been used to decorate swords and knives, including this 13th–16th-century ceremonial obsidian blade from Mexico.

The handle is adorned with small pieces of shell and the mineral turquoise.

The crown's stones include emeralds, sapphires, and pearls.

The cross was added to the crown in the 11th century.

Status
This imperial crown was created in the 10th century for King Otto I of Germany. It was used in coronations of kings of the Holy Roman Empire for more than 800 years.

Medieval coins such as this one were stamped with a symbol of the city or its ruler.

Wealth
Gold and silver have been associated with wealth and prosperity for a long time. Silver was first used as currency more than 5,000 years ago, and gold about 3,000 years later.

This chalcedony and gold ring shows Minerva, a goddess to whom the Romans prayed to grant them good health and wisdom.

This plaque depicts Christ.

Health
The earliest civilizations believed that some stones improved well-being. Today, stones such as ruby, quartz, and garnet are viewed by some as having health-boosting properties.

WHAT TREASURE MEANS TO US

Native elements

Some of Earth's simplest treasures are also the most valuable. Chemical elements that occur in a pure form in nature are called native elements. They include the sparkling riches of gold, silver, and diamonds.

Gold

With a history and an appeal like no other precious metal, nothing compares to gold.

Gold has fascinated humans ever since this rare, shiny yellow metal was first discovered by ancient civilizations around 4000 BCE. Soft enough to be worked without heating, it was soon used for precious things—like gifts to the gods, decorating royal buildings, and later as money. It is as popular and desirable now as it has ever been.

Imperial Roman coins often displayed the emperor's likeness.

Coins and currency
The first gold coins were made in modern-day Türkiye around 640 BCE. Gold makes for an excellent currency because it is valuable and doesn't tarnish or corrode, but cheaper metals, paper, and plastic are used these days.

The more vibrant yellow-orange a gold nugget appears, the higher its pure gold content.

Fool's gold
The mineral pyrite has a similar color and metallic shine to gold, but it is often called "fool's gold." This is because it has tricked many into thinking that they had found the real thing. Pyrite has many uses in the modern world, but it is nowhere near as valuable as gold.

Pyrite is paler than gold, and unlike gold, it tarnishes.

Pyrite can sometimes have angled, crystal-like formations.

22 | NATIVE ELEMENTS

Elaborate jewelery
Ancient peoples crafted gold into delicate jewelery. This breastplate was made by the Scythians of modern-day Iran around the 8th century BCE. It shows the three tiers of Scythian mythology.

The outer tier shows the heavens, the middle tier is the air between, and the innermost tier represents Earth.

Gold fever
In 1848, gold was discovered in California. This led to a "gold rush" as thousands of people migrated to the state, hoping to change their lives by striking gold. In San Francisco alone, the population exploded from 500 people in 1847 to more than 150,000 just five years later.

A man pans for gold in 1850.

A message for our neighbors
The *Voyager 1* and *2* spacecrafts launched in 1977 carried gold disks containing sounds from Earth in the hope of sending a message to aliens. Gold was chosen for its durability, ensuring the disks could withstand the harsh conditions of space for billions of years.

Etchings on the disk show how to play it, and how to find planet Earth.

Buried gold
Some ancient communities buried their dead in fine clothes accompanied by gold ornaments to reflect their status. This spectacular folded gold crown was discovered in a 1st-century CE burial site of the Tillya-tepe people of Afghanistan.

GOLD | 23

River nuggets
Alluvial gold is found in river beds, where it ends up after rain and wind have washed it from seams in rock.

Aztec piercing
The Aztecs (Mexica) of modern-day Mexico were renowned for their skill with gold, which they associated with royalty and status. This serpent's head is a labret—a lip-piercing decoration.

Labrets showed off the wearer's political power, and signaled their breath as precious.

The split tongue could be retracted or moved from side to side.

Getting gold from rock

Not all gold that is discovered is pure in its natural form. Much of the world's gold is found in ore (rock) that contains other metals and elements. The gold is extracted in a process known as smelting, which involves the ore being heated up to a super-high temperature. Chemicals such as mercury and cyanide are used to help separate the now-liquid gold from impurities in the rock.

After it has been separated, liquid gold can be poured into any shape by using a mold.

NATIVE ELEMENTS

Gold bars
Liquid gold shaped into bars is called cast bullion. To qualify as bullion, it needs to be at least 99.5 percent pure.

The weight of the gold is stamped on the bar.

Fine gold is the highest quality of gold.

This bar has 999.99 parts of gold per thousand, which is also known as 24 carat (ct) gold—the most valuable form of gold.

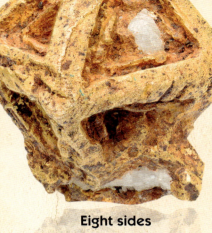

Hard, angled surfaces are typical of octahedral gold.

Eight sides
Some of the world's rarest gold is found in the form of octahedral (eight-faced) crystals. Octahedral gold can be made artificially by scientists using modern technology.

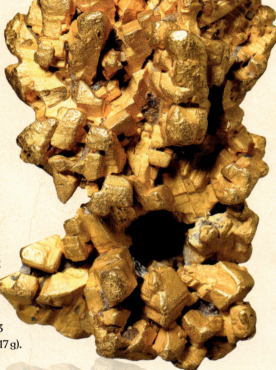

Huge nugget
The Latrobe nugget is one of the largest pieces of cubic gold found to date. It was discovered in Australia in 1853 and weighs 25¼ oz (717 g).

Wire gold is one of the rarest types of gold

Strands of gold run along this striking ⅘-in (2.1-cm) piece.

Wire gold
Pictured here is an especially rare type of the metal known as wire gold. Its long strands formed through unique processes, leading to a shape that resembles a ram's horn.

The richest person in history?
A 14th-century emperor was possibly the richest person who has ever lived—all thanks to gold. Mansa Musa's vast realm in West Africa included huge deposits of gold, which he used to trade with other rulers. The value of his wealth is impossible to know, but estimates put it at many hundreds of billions of dollars—more than any person since.

While on the *hajj* (pilgrimage) in 1324, Mansa Musa gave out so many gifts of gold that he caused its value to drop!

GOLD | 25

Golden place

Gold has long held a sacred place in many religions—and many temples around the world feature it prominently. Among the most striking is the Sri Darbār Sāhib in Amritsar, India—one of the holiest sites of the Sikh religion. The upper floors of the temple are adorned with thin sheets of gold, making it look even more beautiful and special.

Silver

This precious metal has a history stretching back thousands of years, with unique qualities that make it valuable today.

For a long time, silver has been in the shadow of gold—used for many of the same things, such as jewelery and currency, but usually considered less valuable. Silver is mainly found in rocks as ore, and also in its pure, native form—sometimes as stunning wiry crystals. Today, silver's exceptional ability to conduct heat and electricity has made it essential to technologies ranging from computer chips to solar panels. It is also naturally antibacterial, and has been used in medicine and healing for centuries.

Crystal
Silver crystals form in branchlike shapes.

Wire
Unlike the crystal variety, wire silver features irregular, thin strands of the metal.

This silver nugget was found in Kongsberg, Norway, in mines famous for producing very pure silver.

Natural state
Most silver is found in rocks as ore. Only a tiny amount of silver is found in its natural state, often near deposits of gold, copper, or lead.

Nugget
Lumps of silver occur when molten silver cools.

NATIVE ELEMENTS

A mountain of silver

The 16th-century Spanish conquistadors sought riches in South America. While they longed for gold, they primarily found silver. In 1545, the discovery of silver in the Bolivian mountain settlement of Potosí brought huge riches to the Spanish Empire. More silver was extracted from the village than from anywhere else in the world, but thousands of Indigenous people and enslaved Africans died while laboring under brutal conditions in the mines.

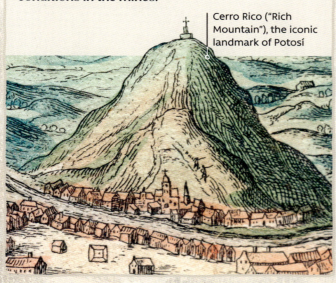

Cerro Rico ("Rich Mountain"), the iconic landmark of Potosí

Precious stones decorate the king's crown and clothes.

Silver's flexibility enabled fine details to be worked into the bust.

Pieces of eight

Silver was taken from South American mines such as those in Potosí, and minted into Spanish dollar coins. These coins became known as "pieces of eight"—they could be physically cut into eight, with each piece used as a smaller unit of currency.

Silver was used for coins because it is soft and long-lasting, though it tarnishes easily.

Fit for a king

Silver busts, like this one of the 13th-century French king Louis IX, were often created to honor royalty. Silver was a popular material because it was easy to work with and shined when polished.

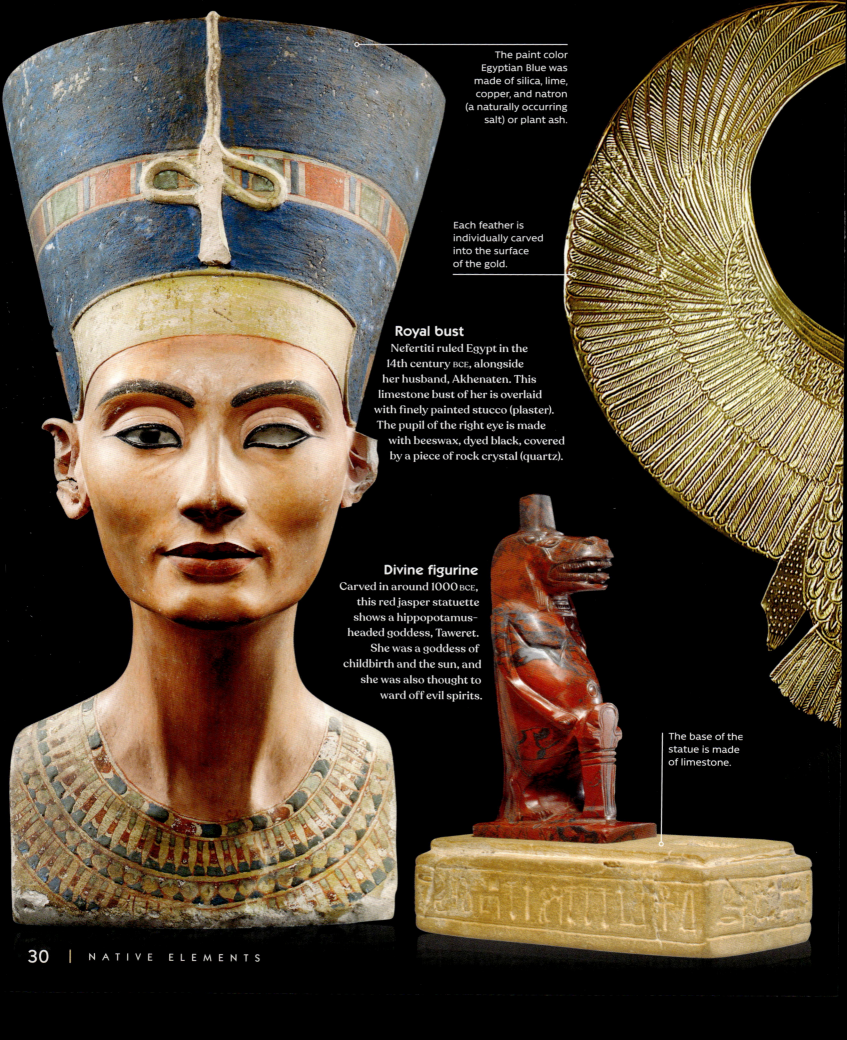

The paint color Egyptian Blue was made of silica, lime, copper, and natron (a naturally occurring salt) or plant ash.

Each feather is individually carved into the surface of the gold.

Royal bust
Nefertiti ruled Egypt in the 14th century BCE, alongside her husband, Akhenaten. This limestone bust of her is overlaid with finely painted stucco (plaster). The pupil of the right eye is made with beeswax, dyed black, covered by a piece of rock crystal (quartz).

Divine figurine
Carved in around 1000 BCE, this red jasper statuette shows a hippopotamus-headed goddess, Taweret. She was a goddess of childbirth and the sun, and she was also thought to ward off evil spirits.

The base of the statue is made of limestone.

30 | NATIVE ELEMENTS

TREASURES OF
ancient Egypt

The art and artifacts of ancient Egypt are among the oldest and finest objects ever made. They were produced over thousands of years, but usually feature the same themes in a consistent style. Gold, lapis lazuli, and other precious gems were used to create pieces that honored the gods and the pharaohs (the rulers of Egypt).

Decorative collar

Formed in the vulture-like shape of the royal protector goddess Nekhbet, this gold collar dates from c.1550–1298 BCE.

Nekhbet holds a shen, the symbol for eternity.

A pharaoh would have had hundreds of shabtis in their burial chamber.

The gold bracelet is inlaid with lapis lazuli and carnelian.

Afterlife attendant

Important people's tombs contained limestone figurines such as this one. Known as shabtis, they show people with particular jobs, such as nurse or a bodyguard, ready to help their master or mistress in the afterlife.

Royal bracelet

This cuff was made for Pharaoh Shoshenq II (r. 887–885 BCE). It shows the healing Eye of Horus, above a hieroglyph (symbol used in writing) called Neb (the checkered basket). Together, they represent eternal protection for the pharaoh.

USHABTI FIGURE OF TA-KAREI

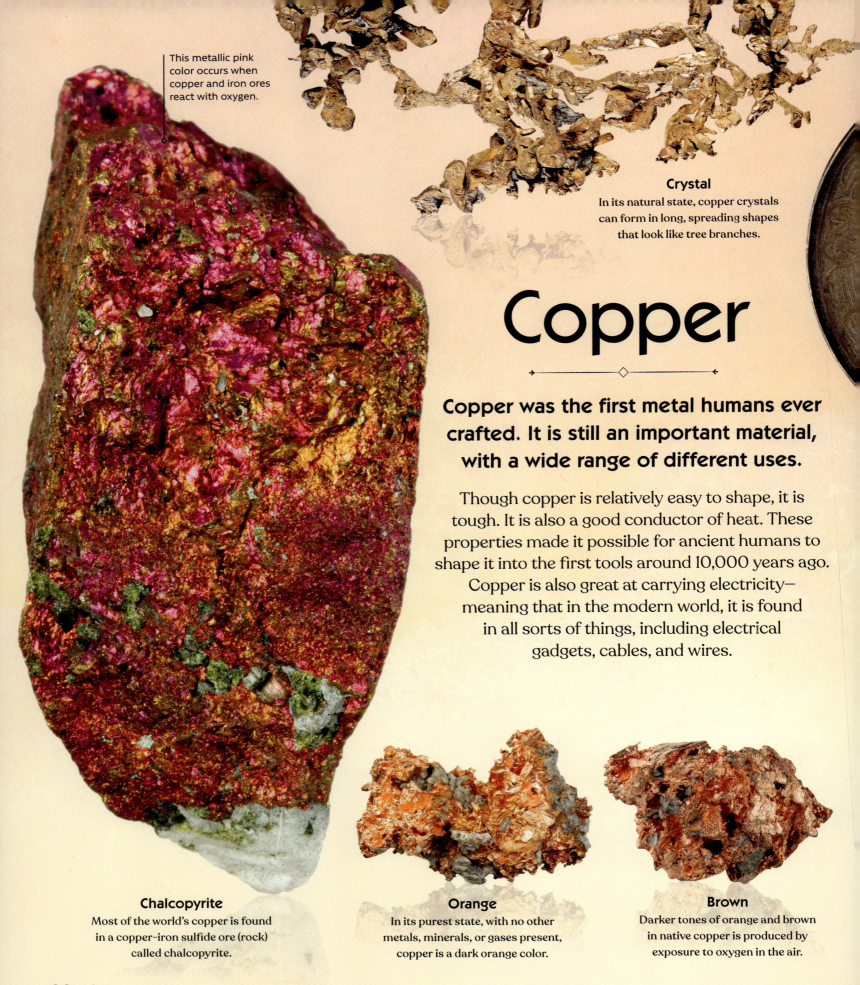

This metallic pink color occurs when copper and iron ores react with oxygen.

Crystal
In its natural state, copper crystals can form in long, spreading shapes that look like tree branches.

Copper

Copper was the first metal humans ever crafted. It is still an important material, with a wide range of different uses.

Though copper is relatively easy to shape, it is tough. It is also a good conductor of heat. These properties made it possible for ancient humans to shape it into the first tools around 10,000 years ago. Copper is also great at carrying electricity—meaning that in the modern world, it is found in all sorts of things, including electrical gadgets, cables, and wires.

Chalcopyrite
Most of the world's copper is found in a copper-iron sulfide ore (rock) called chalcopyrite.

Orange
In its purest state, with no other metals, minerals, or gases present, copper is a dark orange color.

Brown
Darker tones of orange and brown in native copper is produced by exposure to oxygen in the air.

32 | NATIVE ELEMENTS

A copper skin

The Statue of Liberty in New York is made from iron covered in a thin sheet of copper. The metal was chosen because it is more resistant to corrosion than others. However, over time it has reacted to oxygen, and a green patina (film) has developed on its surface.

The copper was orange before oxidization turned it green.

Copper mixed with silver is quite soft, making it easy to mark.

Mixing it up
Copper combines well with other metals or compounds, creating stronger alloys (metal mixtures), such as bronze: a mixture of copper and tin. This 13th–14th-century Syrian bowl is made from a mixture of copper and silver.

The astrolabe's rings and plates could be rotated to find either latitude or the time.

Charting a course
Copper is pliable (easy to mold), which made it ideal for early scientific instruments, such as this 10th-century Islamic astrolabe. This device helped sailors navigate and figure out the time, using the positions of the sun and stars.

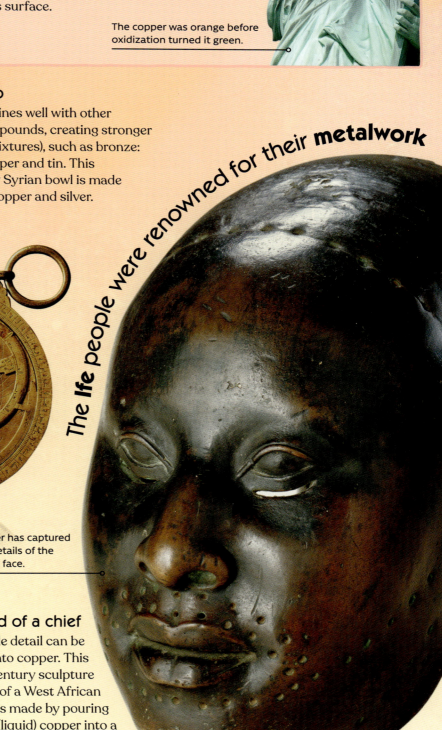

The Ife people were renowned for their metalwork

Ocean wires
Copper conducts electricity well and is resistant to water erosion. This makes it the perfect material for underwater cables. The first transatlantic telegraph cable was made of copper wire in 1858.

Electrical pulses sent along the cable were used to transmit messages between Europe and North America.

Copper has captured fine details of the chief's face.

The head of a chief
Incredible detail can be worked into copper. This 12th–15th-century sculpture of the head of a West African Ife chief was made by pouring molten (liquid) copper into a mold made of wax.

COPPER | 33

Industrial diamonds

Only about 20 percent of diamonds are used in jewelery. Because diamonds are extremely hard, the rest serve various industrial purposes, including sawing, cutting, drilling, and polishing. Some diamonds are crushed into a powder and used in tools to grind things down.

This drill tip is covered in diamond dust.

Rough
Diamonds shine even in their rough form. This yellow stone is one of the world's largest uncut diamonds.

Yellow
Pure diamonds are clear. If there are traces of nitrogen, the diamond will be yellow.

Orange
This is one of the rarest diamond colors. The orange color comes from nitrogen.

Diamond

The hardest mineral on Earth, a diamond can only be scratched by another diamond. Its name comes from the ancient Greek word *adamantos*, which means "invincible."

Diamonds are probably the best-known of all gemstones, famous for their brilliance and the rainbow colors that sparkle out of them when cut. They can be as old as 3.5 billion years, and form under immense pressure, sometimes 500 miles (800 km) deep in Earth. To reach the surface, they must be carried up in magma (molten rock). Diamonds are found in India, Brazil, and South Africa.

Brilliant cut
A brilliant cut has 57–58 facets (faces), which are designed to bounce as much light as possible through a diamond, making it sparkle.

A brilliant cut has a dome on top and a cone shape beneath.

Carbonado
Also known as black diamond, carbonado is very rare and one of the toughest forms of diamond.

34 | NATIVE ELEMENTS

Shining star
The most expensive gemstone ever sold is the Pink Star diamond. It was sold to a Chinese company at auction in 2017, for a staggering $71.2 million (£57 million).

The Pink Star is as big as a strawberry.

The sword's hilt is studded with a series of diamonds.

The Cullinan Diamond
The largest diamond ever found was the Cullinan Diamond. It was as heavy as a basketball, and was mined in South Africa in 1905. It was eventually cut into nine big stones and 96 smaller ones.

The handle features gold and tortoiseshell.

Napoleon's sword
This glittering sword is studded with 42 brilliant-cut diamonds and an exceptionally rare centerpiece diamond known as "the Regent." It was made in 1801 to mark Napoleon Bonaparte becoming First Consul of France, and was used when he became emperor of France in 1804.

This jewel was cut from the Cullinan Diamond.

The Regent is sometimes described as the most beautiful diamond in the world.

Brown
If the structure of a diamond crystal distorts as it forms, the gemstone may become brown.

DIAMOND | 35

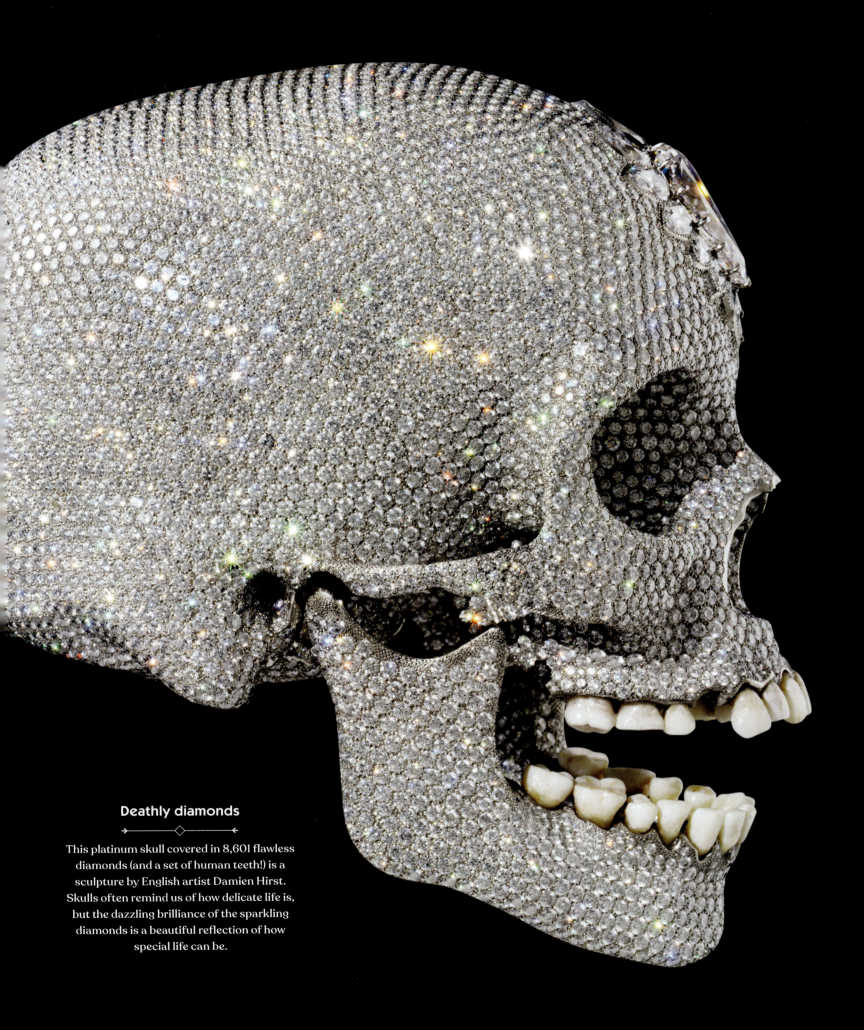

Deathly diamonds

This platinum skull covered in 8,601 flawless diamonds (and a set of human teeth!) is a sculpture by English artist Damien Hirst. Skulls often remind us of how delicate life is, but the dazzling brilliance of the sparkling diamonds is a beautiful reflection of how special life can be.

Gemstones

From the vibrant reds of rubies and lush greens of emeralds to the mesmerizing patterns of agate and malachite, the world of gemstones is rich with treasures that are beautiful, rare, and durable.

Sapphire

Irish poet Oscar Wilde once wrote "the sapphire shall be as blue as the great sea," referring to sapphire's distinctive color.

Sapphire is the blue variety of the mineral corundum and is chiefly made of aluminum and oxygen. Small amounts of other elements create this gem's many dazzling colors. Most sapphires come from Australia, Myanmar (Burma), Madagascar, and Sri Lanka, where they are often found in river beds. After diamond, corundum is the second hardest mineral, which means that sapphires are both beautiful and durable.

Pyramid shapes are typical of sapphire's crystal structure.

Blue sapphire's color is caused by traces of iron and titanium.

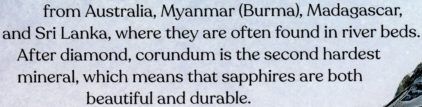

Padparadscha
These pink-orange sapphires take their name from the Sinhalese word for the color of the lotus flower.

Blue
This deep blue sapphire is a rough specimen with imperfections and bands of color on the top right.

Stealing the Star of India

In a daring burglary known as the "Jewel Heist of the Century," the Star of India sapphire was stolen from New York's American Museum of Natural History in 1964. The Star was one of 24 stones taken by a group including Jack Murphy, a surfing champion known as "Murf the Surf." Murphy wasn't an expert thief, but took advantage of lax security, including broken burglar alarms. The Star of India was later found in a bus station locker in Florida.

The Star of India features a star optical effect called an asterism.

Jack Murphy and his accomplices were arrested two days after the heist.

Elaborate cross

This 16th-century cross was made in Russia by skilled artisans, and was worn as a chest decoration. A central sapphire is surrounded by gemstones, a gold and silver setting, enamel, and an outer edge of pearls.

The sapphire is carved in the shape of Jesus Christ on the cross.

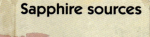

Sapphire sources

• Sapphire mining sites

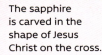

Rough
This rough specimen's color varies from amber to dark caramel and red. Its sides display a glassy sheen.

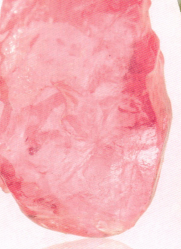

Pink
Chromium impurities create pink tones in sapphires, such as in this uncut specimen.

Colorless
This colorless to creamy white sapphire has a triangular shape and some fractures.

SAPPHIRE | 41

This rough ruby has angled edges and shows some surface cracks.

Ruby

Ancient Indians called ruby the "king of the precious stones," for its rarity and beauty.

Rubies are the red variety of the mineral corundum, making them a relation of sapphires. In fact, the difference between red rubies and pink sapphires is often a matter of opinion, and some ancient Indian and Burmese miners believed that pale pink sapphires were unripe rubies. The stone's red color comes from the mineral chromium, creating gemstones that range from pale rose to deep red. The finest rubies are vivid red in color, with a brightness that makes them glow in sunlight.

Pink
A pink stone indicates only a small amount of chromium, and also iron.

Red
The most prized and valuable rubies are deep crimson red and contain the most chromium.

Tapering crystal
This specimen of crystal ruby is shown with the rock matrix it grew from.

42 | GEMSTONES

Skin deep

Soldiers in ancient Burma (modern-day Myanmar) believed that wearing a ruby close to their heart would grant them protection. This belief in the power of the stone was so strong that legends state that some warriors went as far as cutting their flesh to insert rubies under their skin for extra safety.

Warriors may have inserted rubies in places prone to injury, such as in arms and legs.

Religious rubies

Rubies have been used to decorate religious items—such as this gold-covered book of prayers worn as a pendant—for hundreds of years.

This fingernail-size prayer-book pendant was made in Italy around 1550.

Dazzling star

This rare ruby features a bright star effect caused by the mineral rutile. In the most valuable examples, the star is centered and has six arms of equal length.

Stones with this star effect are often cut and polished as cabochons.

Fit for a queen

This tiara is a replica of a piece that was part of a parure (set) made for the future queen of Sweden to wear at the coronation of French leader Napoleon I in 1804. The parure was later passed on to the Danish royal family, who saw the ruby as the perfect gemstone to match the red in Denmark's national colors.

The rubies are surrounded by diamonds and inlaid in gold.

RUBY | 43

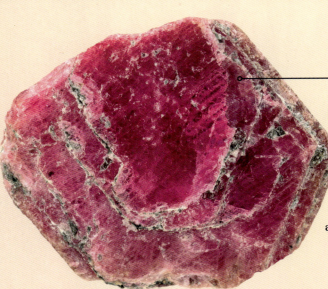

The corundum in ruby naturally forms in rough hexagonal crystals.

Hexagonal crystals
The most common shape for a ruby crystal to form is a flat hexagon. This shape means that cut rubies are most often cushion-shaped or oval, because cutters try to make the most of the shape and waste as little of the stone as possible.

Ancient Hindus offered rubies to the god **Krishna**, believing that it would help them be **reincarnated** as an **emperor**

The dark green crystals in anyolite are either the minerals tschermakite or pargasite.

Anyolite is a rock of **vibrant green zoisite** with **rubies** sprinkled throughout

Rubies mixed with rock are generally not of gem-quality.

Striations (grooves) reflect that the ruby was produced after geological pressure or heat.

Mining ruby
This ruby in a rock matrix was mined in Aust-Agder, Norway. Rough stones can be found in several countries, including Thailand, Sri Lanka, and Myanmar, which is home to the world's finest-quality rubies. Ruby mining is extremely important for Myanmar's economy.

Pigeon-blood red
Some of the most vibrant red rubies are ones that grow in marble. Marble has a low iron content, which results in rubies with an intense color that is known as "pigeon-blood" red by gemologists.

This ruby comes from the "Valley of the Rubies" in Mogok, Myanmar.

Ruby lasers
A ruby is more than just a pretty gemstone. The stone's qualities of strength, ability to absorb heat, and red shine resulted in rubies being used in the first lasers in the 1960s. Rubies have been used in lasers for medicine, precision cutting, and measuring distances. Today, synthetic rubies are used in laser technology.

The ruby is spread irregularly throughout the rock.

When the ruby is stimulated by light, it creates a laser beam.

RUBY | 45

TREASURES OF India

Guardian goddess
Standing 16 in (40 cm) high, this gold and bejeweled statue shows Chamunda, the guardian goddess of Mysuru. As the protector of her city, she holds a variety of weapons in her 16 hands, each one given to her by one of her fellow gods.

This hand holds a club decorated with what may be her victims' heads.

Precious stones adorn the goddess's forehead and clothes.

Indian civilization is at least 5,000 years old. Its cultural heritage embraces Hindu, Buddhist, Muslim, and many other traditions, and all are reflected in its diversity of sacred, royal, and personal treasures. Precious materials such as gold, rubies, emeralds, and diamonds have been used to make dazzling works of art. Sandstone, limestone, and granite rocks have been transformed into beautiful landmarks and temples.

A tassel attached to the handle features many tiny pearls.

Decorative dagger
Made in the early 1900s, this ornamental dagger echoes the style of those created for the Mughals, the Muslim dynasty that ruled India from 1526 to 1857. It features a jade hilt with diamonds and rubies arranged in floral patterns, and a red sheath.

The sheath is made of velvet.

National symbol
Designed to sit on a pillar, the lion capital was one of many carved in the reign of Ashoka, India's great Buddhist emperor, around 250 BCE. The pillars were used to let the public know Ashoka's orders. The lion capital became the country's national symbol in 1950.

The four lions represent power, courage, pride, and confidence.

The Buddhist "wheel of law," or dharmachakra, represents the religion's teachings.

Wedding celebration
At 472 ft (144 m) tall, this is one of 14 *gopura*, or gateways, to the Madurai Meenakshi Sundareswarar Hindu temple in Tamil Nadu. These *gopura* celebrate the wedding of the gods Sundareshwara (or Shiva) to Meenakshi (also called Parvati). They are made of limestone and granite, and were built in the 7th century.

To keep the colors vibrant, the temple's 1,500 god and goddess figures are painted every 12 years.

Bird of paradise
Tipu Sultan ruled the Kingdom of Mysore from 1782 to 1799. This gold and gem-studded mythical Huma bird sculpture was part of his throne. At 16½ in (42 cm) tall, it topped the canopy under which the Muslim ruler sat.

Rubies, diamonds, and emeralds adorn the feathers and body.

TREASURES OF INDIA | 47

Spinel

Treasured for its famous luster when polished, spinel is a relatively rare gemstone.

Spinel is composed of magnesium aluminum oxide, and appears in many colors. It is most sought-after in a blood-red shade known as "ruby spinel." Its structure means that it reflects light with a particular brilliance, in a similar way to diamonds and garnets. Super-rare "star" spinel is especially sparkly. Spinel is found in Myanmar (Burma), Sri Lanka, Madagascar, Afghanistan, Pakistan, and Australia, often in river beds.

Crystal clusters
Spinels are usually found as individual crystals and stones, but can also form clusters like this one.

Natural crystals often have a dull, glassy sheen.

Spinel crystals are usually octahedral (eight-sided).

In rock
Spinel crystals grow inside magnesium-rich igneous rock, developing as lava cools and solidifies.

Blue
Pure spinel is colorless, but minerals in the crystals can add color. Here, cobalt has turned the spinel blue.

Black
Pleonast (black spinel) gets its deep, highly reflective color from iron. This variety of spinel is very rare.

Pink
Chromium makes spinel pink. The more chromium present, the more vibrant the pink hue.

Pointing the way
Magnetite (or lodestone) is a member of the spinel group of minerals. It is magnetic, which means a pointer shaped from magnetite will always point in the same direction. Because of this, it was used to make the needles of early compasses, helping sailors find their way.

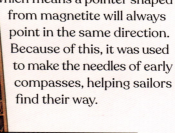

Chinese compass with magnetite needle

Each half of the crown is lined with 37 pearls.

Nearly 5,000 diamonds are set in decorative patterns around the crown.

Fit for an empress
The imperial crown of Catherine the Great (r. 1762–1796) is one of Russia's most valuable treasures. Its centerpiece is the "balas ruby," which is actually the second-largest spinel in the world, and weighs more than a golf ball.

SPINEL | 49

Sculpture ornament
This 17th–19th century Nepalese-Tibetan headpiece features turquoise Buddhas at either end. It was made to sit on the forehead of a sculpture.

Its lavish design features turquoise, gold, diamonds, coral, rubies, emeralds, lapis lazuli, sapphires, and garnet.

Rough
Turquoise forms in seams or thin crusts, as stalactites, or in clumps of rounded nodules, as is the case here.

Tlaloc's eyes are made of turquoise.

Rain god
Turquoise, stone, shell, and coral combine in this mask of Tlaloc, the rain god of the Mixtec who lived in Mexico. The mask was made between 1300 and 1500.

Turquoise

This scarce blue-green mineral is formed from copper and aluminum phosphate.

Turquoise was one of the first gems to be mined, and archaeologists have found turquoise beads in modern-day Iraq that are more than 7,000 years old. Many ancient cultures, including those of Egypt and Persia (modern-day Iran), regarded it as sacred.

Turquoise encased in sandstone

The figures surrounding the lute player are probably the audience.

Mixed origins
Turquoise is found among both sedimentary rocks, such as limestone, and volcanic rocks, including basalt.

Lute player
This 12th–13th century turquoise-glazed stone bowl showing a lute player was probably made in Persia.

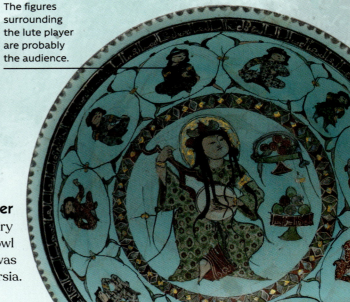

50 | GEMSTONES

Mineral composition
Azurite's crystalline structure takes more than 40 forms, including columns, hexagons, fibers, and prisms.

Polishing enhances the mineral's deep blue luster.

Spots of malachite

In this specimen, the large azurite crystals are deep blue and tightly clustered together.

Special stone
Rubbing azurite with moist fine-grain sandpaper produces a smooth, glassy finish.

Azurite

This blue mineral is brittle and can be hard to work with.

Azurite forms when deposits of copper are exposed to air and carbon-dioxide-rich water. It has been used since the time of ancient Egypt to make beads, jewelery, and ornaments. When ground up, azurite can also be used as a paint pigment and to produce dye.

To dye for
During the Ming (1368–1644) and Qing (1644–1911) dynasties, robe makers made dyes from azurite. They achieved this by crushing the mineral, before washing it in water or vinegar to remove impurities.

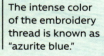

The intense color of the embroidery thread is known as "azurite blue."

Found together
The bright green mineral malachite is often found next to azurite. This is because malachite is actually azurite that has been exposed to air and water and absorbed more copper.

Green malachite stripes alternate with blue bands of azurite.

TURQUOISE AND AZURITE | 51

Malachite

Identifiable by its striking green color that appears in a variety of shades, malachite is both a beautiful gemstone and an important source of copper.

Malachite forms where copper deposits in porous rocks such as limestone are weathered and dissolved in water—the gemstone can be smelted to extract pure copper. It typically appears in grapelike ("botryoidal") clusters, stalactites and stalagmites, fibers, seams, and, occasionally, crystals. Malachite is also a precious stone, and is often used to make jewelery and ornaments.

Malachite's blooms and swirls are formed by copper-infused liquid filtering through the host rock.

Geologists still don't know for sure why malachite is often arranged in distinctive bands within a rock.

Swirling patterns
When seen in cross section, rocks containing malachite display swirling and sometimes smokelike patterns that depend on how the specimen has formed.

52 | GEMSTONES

The Malachite Maid

In Slavic folklore, the Mistress of the Copper Mountain, also called the Malachite Maid, is a mystical being said to live in the depths of Russia's Ural Mountains. She is usually portrayed as a beautiful, green-eyed woman with copper hair, and miners must ask her approval before they begin to extract Earth's riches.

The Malachite Maid's gown is said to be woven with malachite.

Mask of the Red Queen

Dating from 672, this funerary mask is from the Tomb of the Red Queen in the ancient Maya city of Palenque (in modern-day Mexico). The use of malachite for such an important piece shows how highly the Maya thought of this precious material.

Threadlike filaments

Death and rebirth

The paint on the face of this mummy case was made from powdered malachite. To the ancient Egyptians, malachite symbolized death and rebirth. They even called the paradise in the afterlife the "Field of Malachite."

Malachite stalagmites are usually finger-shaped.

Fibrous strands

When it forms into fibrous strands, malachite has a smooth, silky appearance and a deep green color.

This case was made in the 7th century BCE.

Up and down

In caves and underground chambers, malachite-rich dripping water hardens into stalactites that grow down from the ceiling, and rounded botryoidal stalagmites that grow up from the floor.

Quartz

The ancient Greeks described transparent quartz crystals as "eternal ice," and believed it came down from the heavens.

Quartz is one of the most common minerals on Earth, and an ingredient of most rocks. Quartz crystals have well-defined, angular shapes. They typically form in igneous rocks, as well as in cavities inside rocks. There are hundreds of varieties of quartz, including colorless, large crystals and colorful, banded gems with tiny crystals. Quartz gemstones are highly sought-after as jewels, talismans, and decorations.

Quartz "diamonds"

These shiny quartz crystals have natural, well-formed faces and look a bit like diamonds. Known as "Herkimer diamonds," they are found in a few places around the world, including in Herkimer County, New York. Herkimer diamonds are thought to have formed in cavities on the sea floor about 500 million years ago.

Colorless quartz is also called "rock crystal."

Hexagonal crystals, topped by pyramids with six sides

Natural crystal
When quartz has room and time to grow, it naturally forms large, well-defined crystals.

Mysterious skull
This skull is made of quartz and is housed in the British Museum, London, UK. It was once believed to have been made by Aztec craftspeople, but nobody knows its true origins.

This crystal sphere is 10 in (25.4 cm) wide

Quartz is made of silicon and oxygen

Fortune telling
Throughout history, giant quartz crystals have been carved to make crystal balls for fortune tellers. This crystal from Myanmar (Burma) was cut and polished into a sphere in China.

The crystals gleam as they catch the light.

Long, milky white quartz crystals

Crystal cluster
Clear, shiny quartz crystals are a common, relatively cheap, and very popular gemstone.

Pyrite and quartz
This specimen from Peru contains cube-shaped pyrite or "fool's gold," as well as clusters of quartz.

QUARTZ | 55

Geode
These sparkling quartz crystals have formed a geode: a rock cavity lined with crystals.

Microscopic quartz crystals form inside a border of banded agate.

Some of the world's best quartz crystals grow inside geodes

Telling the time
When a small electrical charge is applied to a quartz crystal, the crystal will slightly bend or compress, in a process called oscillation. In fact, quartz oscillation is so regular that it can work as a highly accurate timer, and so quartz is used to make oscillators in watches.

The quartz crystal sits inside the cylinder-shaped oscillator.

Inside view of a quartz watch

Smoky
This brown variety of quartz is called smoky quartz. It gets its color from natural underground radiation.

Citrine
Brownish pyramid-shaped quartz crystals are called citrine. They get their color from iron oxide.

Long, pink tourmaline crystals

Tourmaline in quartz
Here, pink tourmaline quartz crystals have formed inside a mass of white quartz crystals with poorly defined shapes.

Pink geode
This dazzling geode contains small, sparkling quartz crystals. Its color is unnatural, created by dying the quartz.

Rutile is a mineral that usually forms **needlelike** crystals

Rutile-bearing quartz
This quartz variety contains the titanium mineral rutile, which has formed needlelike shapes inside the crystal.

Golden-colored rutile needles can be seen through the faces of the crystal.

QUARTZ | 57

Crystal clear

Light shimmers through the quartz rock crystal chandeliers in the Hall of Mirrors at the Palace of Versailles in France. Illuminated by the glow of 1,000 candles, the 43 chandeliers work with 357 mirrors to capture and disperse light in a dazzling display. They were the height of fashion and very expensive when installed in 1770.

Geode
When amethyst forms as crystals lining cavities or spaces inside rocks, the formation is called a geode. Some geodes are so large people can step inside them.

Chevron zonation
When amethysts are cut in particular directions, they display V-shaped patterns called chevron zonation.

Brazilian
Brazil is a major producer of amethysts that are typically light purple in color.

Amethyst

Tiny amounts of iron give this variety of quartz its distinctive purple color.

Amethyst, a mineral made from a combination of oxygen and silicon, is one of the most precious quartz varieties. In addition to its striking color, amethyst is recognizable by its large crystals. It can form in many geological settings, including inside and on top of igneous rocks and near hot fluids in Earth's crust.

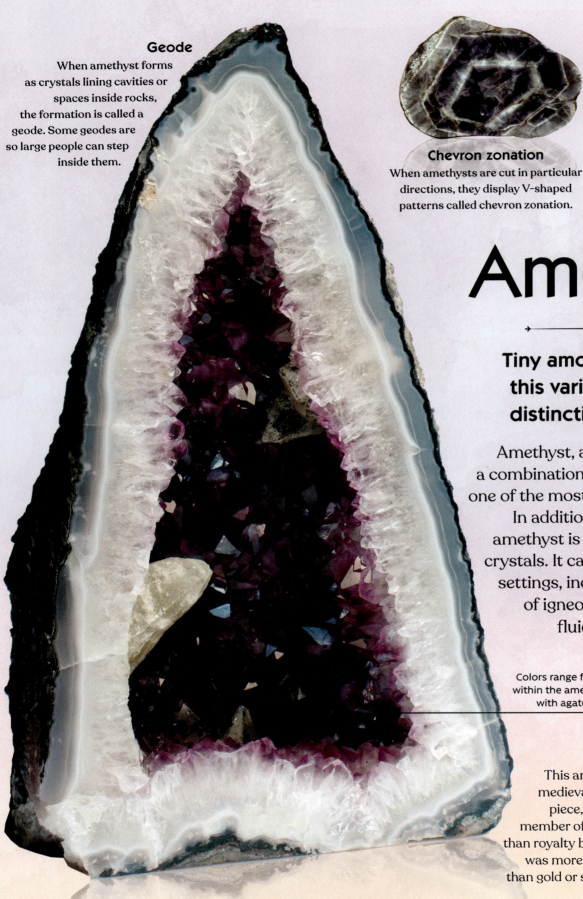

Colors range from purple to white within the amethyst, which is lined with agate on its outer edges.

Affordable beauty
This amethyst necklace originates from medieval Germany. While it is a beautiful piece, it is likely to have been worn by a member of the common folk rather than royalty because amethyst was more affordable than gold or silver.

Ametrine
In ametrine, purple bands of amethyst sit alongside yellow bands of citrine, a yellow variety of quartz.

Faceted and polished
This gemstone has been cut into many faces and polished to show off its natural purple hues.

Yellow prasiolite
This yellow variety of quartz is called prasiolite. It is produced by heating amethyst.

Green prasiolite
Prasiolite can also be green—ranging from light green, as here, to deeper olive greens.

Facets are created by cutting and polishing the stone into flat surfaces called faces, which act as mirrors.

Concave carvings on facets create optical illusions.

A cursed amethyst
The Delhi Purple Sapphire is thought to have been looted from a temple in India. It was brought to England by a Bengal cavalryman, who later came to ruin. Ever since, it has brought bad luck to everyone who has come close to it—and is sometimes called the "Gem of Sorrow."

The gemstone is an amethyst and not a sapphire at all.

Ultramodern cut
This ametrine is cut in a unique way that combines faceting with carving, leading to intriguing patterns and visual effects.

The amount of iron in amethyst determines how intense the purple color is.

Crystals
If they have space and time to grow, individual crystals can form spectacular hexagonal shapes.

Amethyst was a symbol of piety (religious faith) in medieval Europe.

AMETHYST | 61

Chalcedony

Tough, with a huge range of beautiful color patterns, chalcedony has always been one of the most widely used gems.

Chalcedony is a type of quartz, with crystals so tiny that they can only be seen with a microscope. These tiny crystals give a smooth, porcelain-like appearance. Chalcedony can be pink, blue, green, yellow, white, or brown, and some varieties have pretty patterns. It forms in cavities and veins in igneous and sedimentary rocks, and has been used to make everything from arrowheads to intricate jewelery.

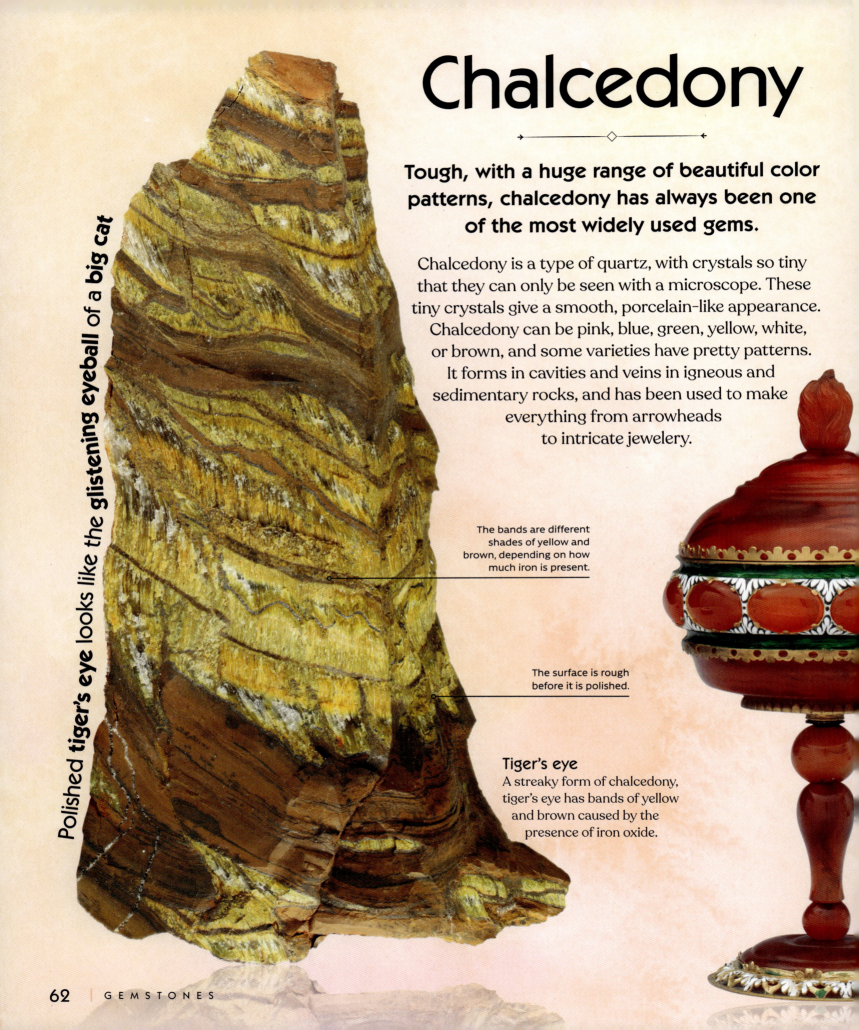

Polished tiger's eye looks like the glistening eyeball of a big cat

The bands are different shades of yellow and brown, depending on how much iron is present.

The surface is rough before it is polished.

Tiger's eye
A streaky form of chalcedony, tiger's eye has bands of yellow and brown caused by the presence of iron oxide.

62 | GEMSTONES

Petrified wood

When a tree dies, its wood can be replaced by minerals, such as chalcedony. This occurs when the wood is quickly buried before it decays, allowing mineral-rich water to fill the spaces between and within the wood cells. Over time, the minerals gradually replace the wood, and sometimes entire forests can be preserved in this way.

Blue chalcedony has replaced the original wood of this 50-million-year-old tree.

A gold lid tops the vase.

Sardonyx vase

This elaborate 16th-century French vase is made of sardonyx: a mixture of onyx and sard. Onyx is a variety of chalcedony that has bands of black and white, while sard is a yellow or brownish type of chalcedony.

Sardonyx has bold colors and banding.

Royal cup

This cup is a royal treasure from the reign of the French king Louis XIV (r. 1643–1715). It is fashioned from a reddish variety of chalcedony called carnelian, and decorated with gold and enamel.

Twelve carnelian cabochons ring the cup.

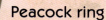

Peacock ring

The focus of this gold ring is a peacock carved into red chalcedony. The ring is thought to come from the ancient city of Seleucia, in modern-day Iraq.

Rounded masses of carnelian

Carnelian
This blood-red variety of chalcedony gets its color from traces of iron oxide.

This gemstone has been cut to show off its pale blue and violet colors.

Rose
This blue and pinkish variety of chalcedony is known as a chalcedony rose.

CHALCEDONY | 63

Botryoidal
Chalcedony is often found in botryoidal form, which means it is shaped like a bunch of grapes.

Long crystals
The quartz crystals that make up chalcedony can sometimes form long, stretched-out structures.

White
This chalcedony pebble is white and cloudy, with some yellow staining.

The top row shows gods and past emperors.

The middle row shows Tiberius and his family.

Praising emperors
This cameo was sculpted into five layers of sardonyx. It was carved during the reign of the Roman emperor Tiberius (r. 14 CE–37 CE), and features 24 figures celebrating the greatness of Roman emperors.

This is the **largest** surviving ancient cameo sculpture

CHALCEDONY | 65

TREASURES OF ancient Greece and Rome

Funeral mask
Unearthed in Greece, this funeral mask was made in around 1500 BCE. Its features were hammered into the gold from the back of the mask, a technique called *repoussé*.

The mask is made from a single sheet of gold, hammered very thin.

The carved figure is a young woman, possibly the wife of an emperor.

Carnelian intaglio
Intaglios are intricately carved gems that can be used with hot wax to create a seal. Carnelian is beautiful, but it is also hard and durable. This makes it perfect for carving designs into without them getting worn away.

Scales have been carefully carved into the gold.

Snake bracelet
Snakes were important symbols for the Romans, representing rebirth, fertility, and healing. This gold bracelet found at Pompeii, Italy, depicts a coiled snake.

Ancient Greek and Roman art have a lot in common. Both cultures created art to honor the gods, and both used lots of gold and marble, with sophisticated pieces designed to be shown off in public places. Once Rome became an empire, ruled by emperors, Roman arts and crafts became more political, celebrating the emperor and other leaders alongside the gods.

Carvings on Augustus's breastplate celebrate the emperor's military victories.

Golden necklace
This intricate necklace is made of gold wire with beads of amethyst and emerald. It was found in Cyprus and dates from 300–100 BCE, which was during the Hellenistic era.

The gold wire has been carefully woven into delicate shapes.

The Augustus of Prima Porta
Standing at an impressive 6 ft 6 in (2 m) tall, this marble statue is of Rome's first emperor, Augustus. It was originally painted in lifelike colors, and shows a youthful Augustus barefoot in a heroic pose, like a god.

The mosaic tiles are stuck down using a thin layer of cement.

Roman mosaic
Wealthy Romans decorated their floors with patterns of tiny tiles, called mosaics. This example is from the city of Rome itself. Its tiles are made of marble and limestone, arranged to show two gladiators engaged in a fight to the death.

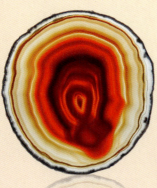

Slice
Color bands can be seen when agate is cut into thin slices.

Brazilian
This specimen is lined with quartz crystals at the edge, and caramel agate bands inside.

Moss
These "moss" patterns are due to staining from manganese oxides and chlorite.

Coyamito
Coyamito is a Mexican region where c. 38-million-year-old agates are found.

Agate is a form of **chalcedony**, which is a type of **quartz**

Agua Nueva
Agates from Agua Nueva Ranch, Chihuahua, Mexico, are known for their intricate patterns and vibrant colors.

Bands follow the outline of the cavity in which the agate formed.

Agate

A variety of quartz with crystals so small they are invisible to the naked eye, agate comes in a wonderful range of colors.

Agate forms when mineral-rich fluids leave silica in rock, which typically happens inside cavities created by gas bubbles in cooling lava. Traces of iron, manganese, and other chemicals are responsible for the array of colors that agates come in, and this gemstone's microcrystals give it a distinctive smooth feel.

At the center
Dating back to the late Bronze Age (1550–1050 BCE), this necklace features a central agate bead, with beads made of gold and the mineral carnelian on either side.

Carnelian is a variety of chalcedony, just like agate.

Portrait of a king
This agate stamp is a cameo of Persian king Kavadh I (r. 488–496 CE). This cameo was made to communicate the king's power.

Thunder eggs
Spherical stones called thunder eggs form inside volcanic rocks such as rhyolites. These stones reveal surprising patterns when split, such as this colorful agate, with blue bands and a central hollow.

The colors formed layer by layer over time.

Islamic seal
This agate object may have been used as an amulet, as well as being used as a seal. It is decorated with an elaborate Naskh inscription, an early Islamic script.

Cursive Arabic calligraphy is carved into the agate.

Banding is visible behind the inscription.

Runic ring
Adorned with an inscription in runic (an ancient Germanic alphabet) around the outside, this agate ring dates back to the 8th–10th centuries. Such rings may have been attached to swords, in the hope of bringing protection to its owner.

Decorative bowl
Carved from moss agate, this bowl has delicate, fernlike inclusions inside it. The bowl's shape is curved and irregular, mirroring the patterns of the agate impurities.

AGATE | 69

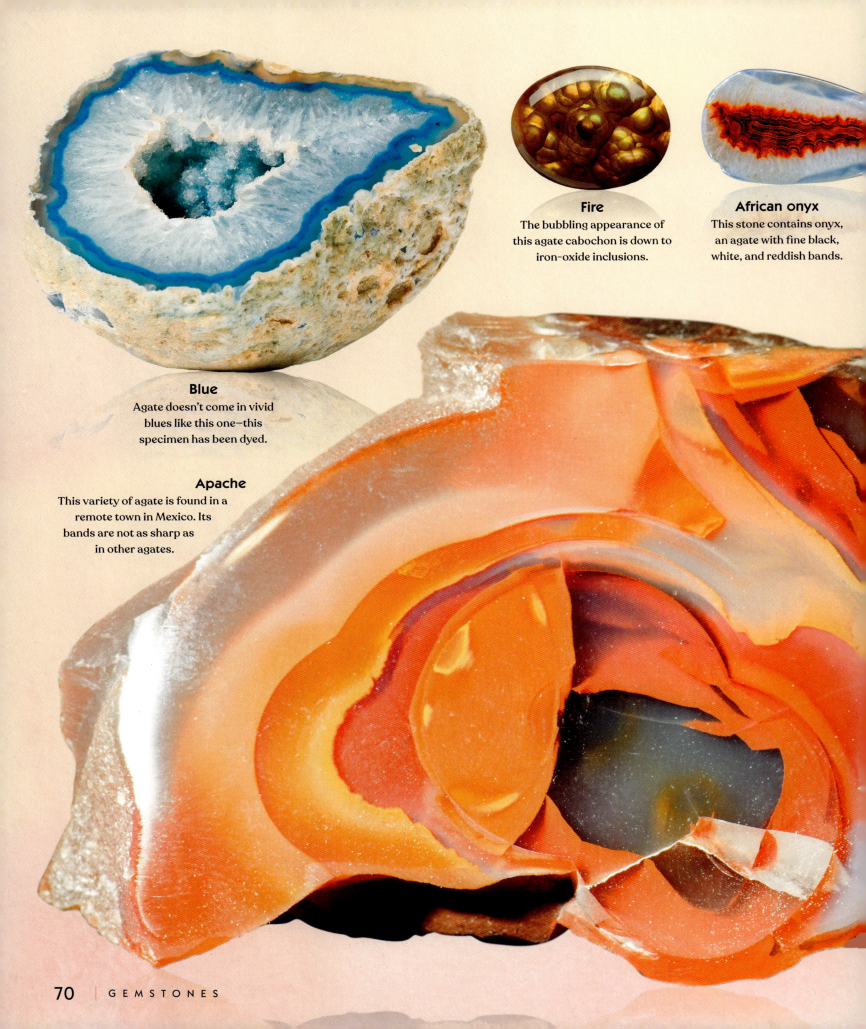

Fire
The bubbling appearance of this agate cabochon is down to iron-oxide inclusions.

African onyx
This stone contains onyx, an agate with fine black, white, and reddish bands.

Blue
Agate doesn't come in vivid blues like this one—this specimen has been dyed.

Apache
This variety of agate is found in a remote town in Mexico. Its bands are not as sharp as in other agates.

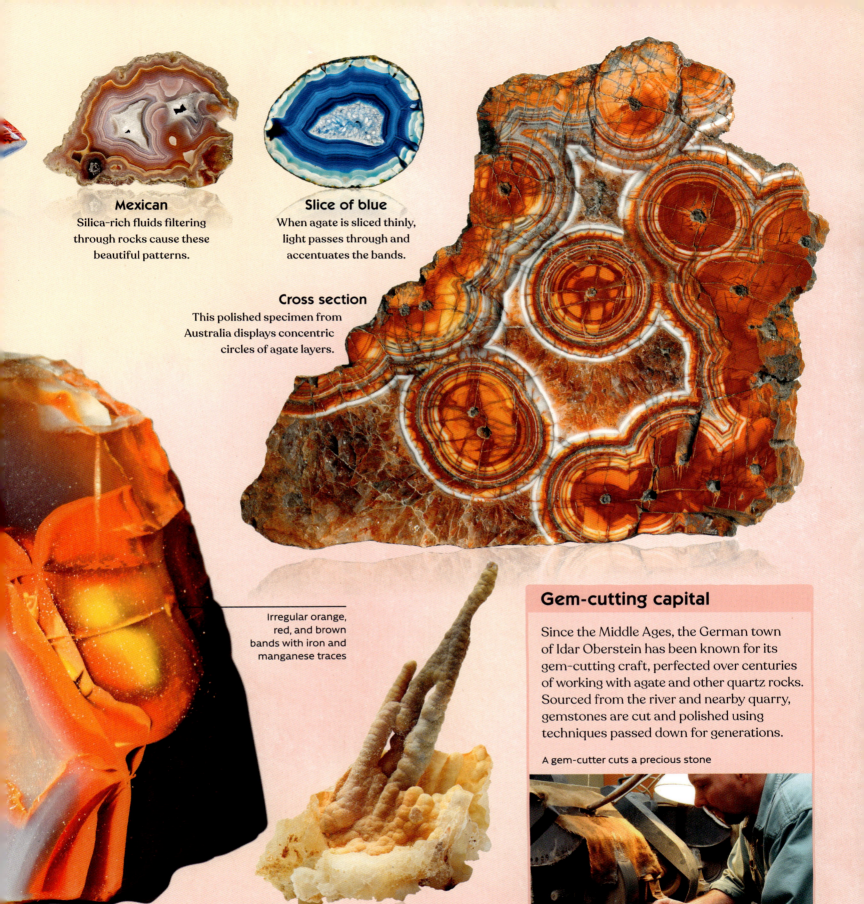

Mexican
Silica-rich fluids filtering through rocks cause these beautiful patterns.

Slice of blue
When agate is sliced thinly, light passes through and accentuates the bands.

Cross section
This polished specimen from Australia displays concentric circles of agate layers.

Irregular orange, red, and brown bands with iron and manganese traces

Bamboo agate
Here, silica-rich waters have solidified into tubelike, stalactite shapes, a bit like bamboo shoots.

Gem-cutting capital

Since the Middle Ages, the German town of Idar Oberstein has been known for its gem-cutting craft, perfected over centuries of working with agate and other quartz rocks. Sourced from the river and nearby quarry, gemstones are cut and polished using techniques passed down for generations.

A gem-cutter cuts a precious stone

AGATE | 71

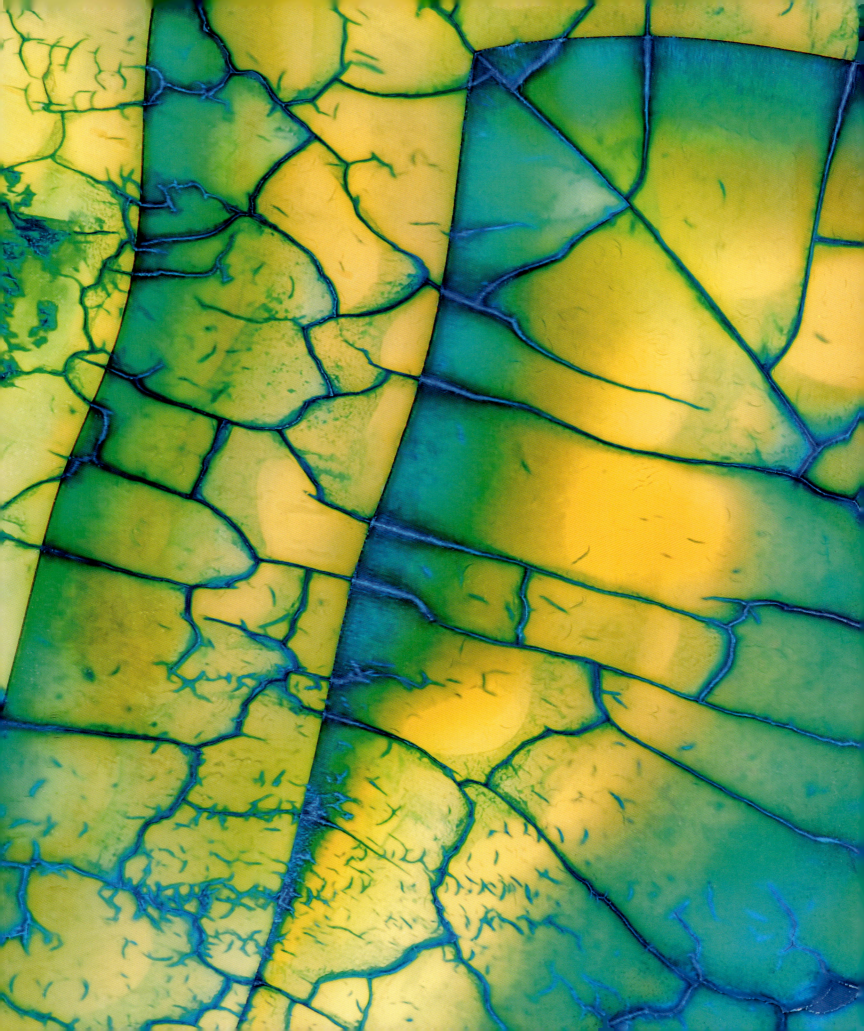

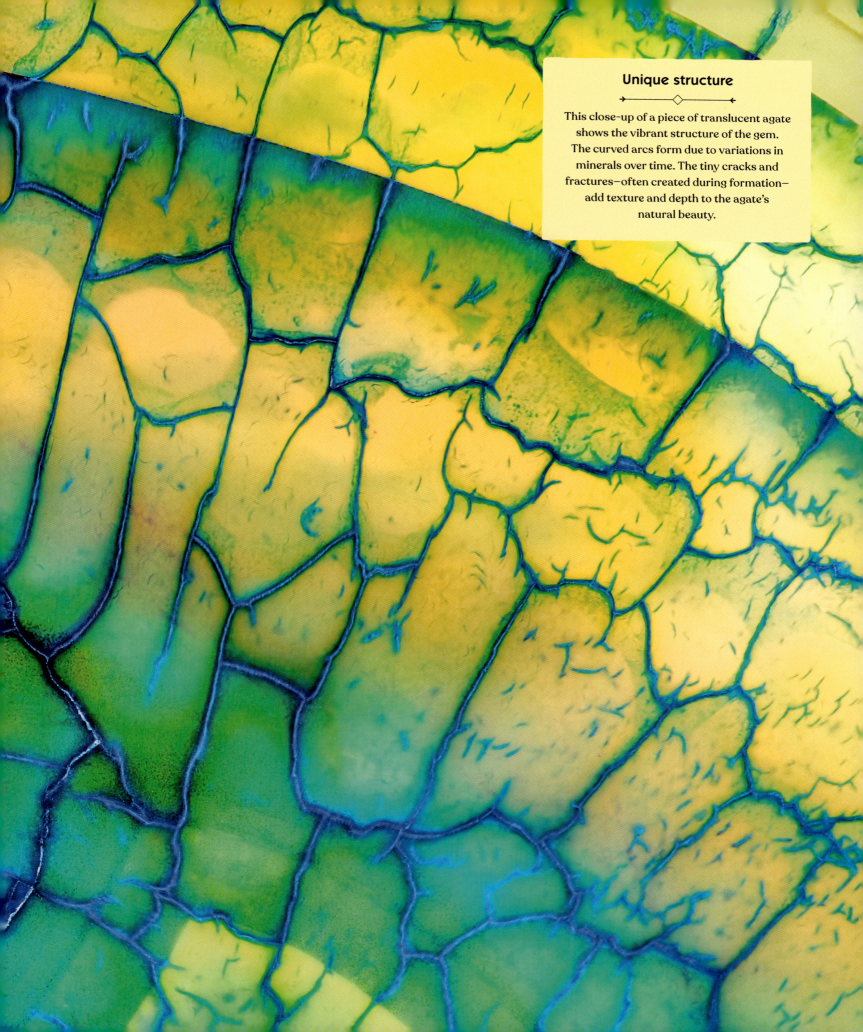

Unique structure

This close-up of a piece of translucent agate shows the vibrant structure of the gem. The curved arcs form due to variations in minerals over time. The tiny cracks and fractures—often created during formation—add texture and depth to the agate's natural beauty.

Jasper

The blood-like color of red jasper attracted the ancient Egyptians, who saw it as a powerful symbol of life and longevity.

Jasper is an opaque (not see-through) variety of chalcedony and consists of microscopic, tightly packed grains. Although it is often red, jasper can be found in a wide array of bold, bright colors thanks to chemical impurities. It forms in metamorphic and sedimentary rocks, and in cavities and veins inside volcanic rocks.

Color bands
This jasper variety from Western Australia, known as mookaite, contains bands of different colors.

Mookaite
Swirling colors of bright yellow and red to pale brown are typical of mookaite.

Red
One of the most common varieties, this red jasper is cut by a thin white vein.

From the **Old French jaspre**, which means *"speckled stone"*

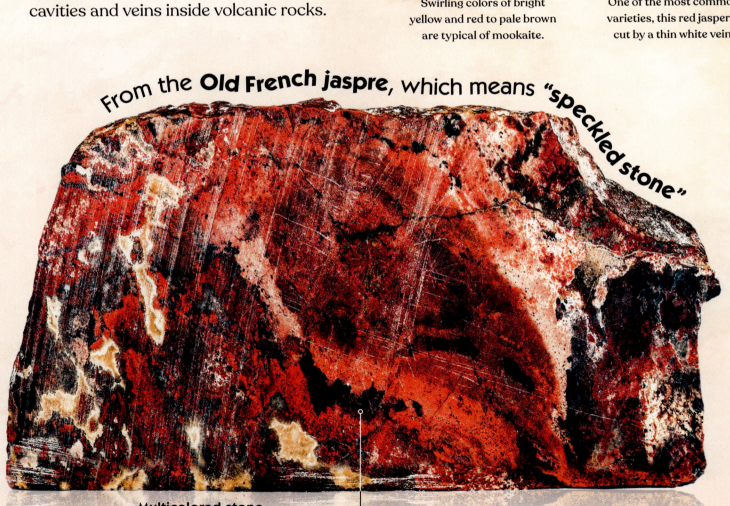

Multicolored stone
The striking red and yellow colors in jasper are typically caused by iron-oxide impurities.

The darker areas, such as this black region, contain more iron.

74 | GEMSTONES

The anteater's eyes are made of diamonds.

The microscopic grains in jasper's makeup mean it is able to hold fine details, such as the anteater's hair.

This artifact is small enough to fit in the palm of your hand.

Collectible animals
This jasper anteater was made by Russian carvers around 1900. Animal figurines such as this were popular and collected by many rich people, including royalty.

Playing games
This leopard head, delicately carved from red jasper, is thought to have been used to play board games in ancient Egypt (c. 1479–1458 BCE).

This piece was probably used to play the popular games Senet and Twenty Squares.

This 2¾-in- (7-cm-) long arrowhead was found in North Africa.

Tools and weapons
Jasper's hardness and ability to be shaped made it ideal for tools and weapons in Neolithic times (c. 10,000–c. 2200 BCE).

Ancient seal

This jasper cylinder seal dates back to the Assyrian period (1300–1200 BCE) and was found in Nineveh, in modern-day Iraq. It was used as a rolling tool to create an impression on soft material such as wet clay. Jasper is durable enough to be used again and again without breaking, and can be carved to show fine details, such as this scene of a ruler, attendants, and animals.

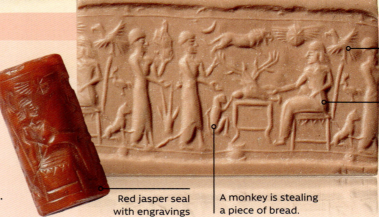

Red jasper seal with engravings

A monkey is stealing a piece of bread.

A bird of prey is landing on the ruler's chair.

The seated ruler is presented with the head of a stag by his attendants.

JASPER | 75

Leopard
This variety of jasper is orbicular, with tiny spherical rings that resemble a leopard's pattern.

Picture
This variety of jasper shows layers that resemble scenery and landscapes.

Yellow
Polished yellow jasper with circular patterns give this specimen a speckled appearance.

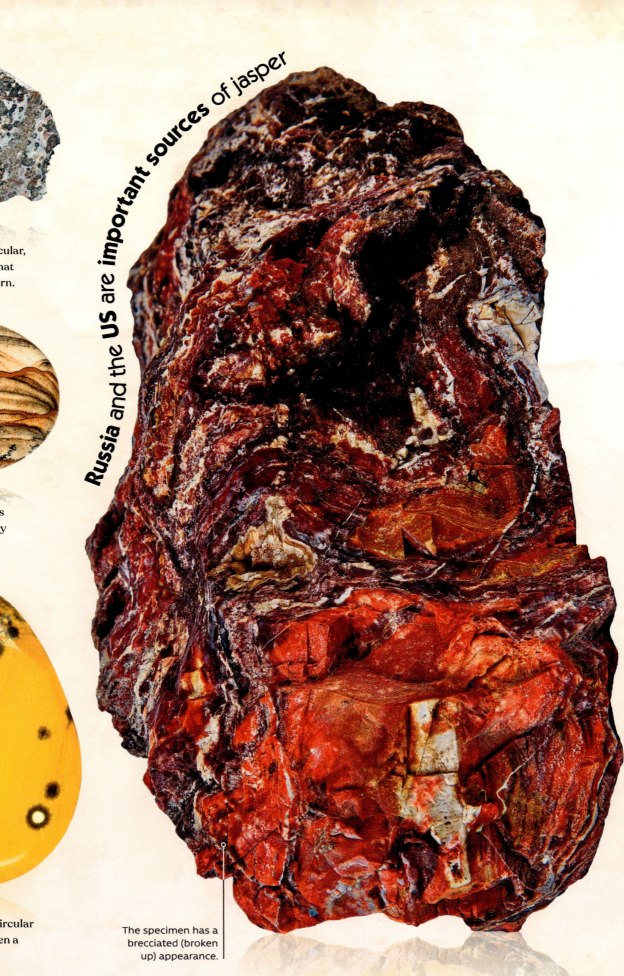

Russia and the **US** are important sources of jasper

The specimen has a brecciated (broken up) appearance.

JASPER | 77

Ancient stripes

Layers of red jasper alternate with stripes of dark iron oxide and yellow tiger's eye in this cross-section of a chunk of rock. Known as a Banded Iron Formation (BIF), this rock was laid down more than 2 BYA, when the first continents were forming on our planet. Originally horizontal, the folding of the layers shows the extreme tectonic forces to which they were subjected.

The horse, lid, and handle are covered in a thin layer of gold.

Horse power
This Tang Era (618–908) silver flask was shaped to resemble a leather bag. Horses were important to the Tang, and symbolized wealth and power.

The mask was made by hammering a sheet of silver into shape.

Loopholes along the sides may have been used to tie the item around an arm.

Jade dragon
This 10th–11th-century dragon plaque is just 4½ in (11.4 cm) long. In Chinese culture, dragons embody imperial power and wisdom, while jade is thought to bring good fortune.

Death mask
This silver death mask was made by the Liao, who ruled northern China from 900 to 1125. It would have been attached to a sheet made of gold, silver, or copper wire.

Turquoise and bronze
This item was made by China's early Erlitou Culture (c. 1900–1500 BCE). It features a bronze base, into which rectangles of turquoise have been placed. The object's purpose is uncertain, but it may have been worn by a shaman during religious rites.

The dragons are made from gold wire and are soldered into place.

The entire body, including the feet, is covered with intricately carved patterns.

The headdress features more than 100 rubies and sapphires, and around 3,500 pearls.

Strings of pearls hang from both sides of the headdress.

Phoenix crown
This ceremonial "phoenix crown" was worn by a Ming empress, Xiaoduan (d.1620). Three golden dragons represent the emperor, while two phoenixes, decorated with kingfisher feathers, symbolize the empress.

TREASURES OF
China

China has produced jewelery and ornamental objects for thousands of years. Many of these items were designed to glorify its powerful imperial dynasties. However, there is also a rich tradition of art that celebrates China's natural history, culture, and religious and mythological beliefs.

Light is diffracted through spheres of silica inside the opal, resulting in colorful displays.

Living underground
The Australian desert town of Coober Pedy sits on the world's largest source of opal. Miners avoid the punishing daytime heat by living underground.

Sandstone is relatively soft and easy to dig into.

The bedrooms can be 26 ft (8 m) below ground level.

Summer temperatures on the surface reach 126°F (52°C).

The vibrant colors stand out against the opal's black background.

Opal

This shimmering stone shows an array of shifting colors.

Unlike most minerals, opal doesn't form well-defined crystals. It is a mix of silica—a mineral made of oxygen and silicon—and water, and usually forms inside sedimentary rocks, in cavities of volcanic rocks, and around hot springs. Prized for its rainbowlike play of colour since ancient Roman times, opal is thought to take its name from the Sanskrit word *upala*, meaning "precious stone."

Black
Precious opals such as this one contain tiny, uniform, closely packed silica spheres that produce its unique color display.

Ethiopian
Opals from Ethiopia are renowned for their color play, as light breaks into separate colors.

Yowah
Opals from the Yowah area of Queensland, Australia, can be up to 7⅞ in (20 cm) across.

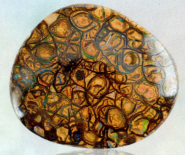

82 | GEMSTONES

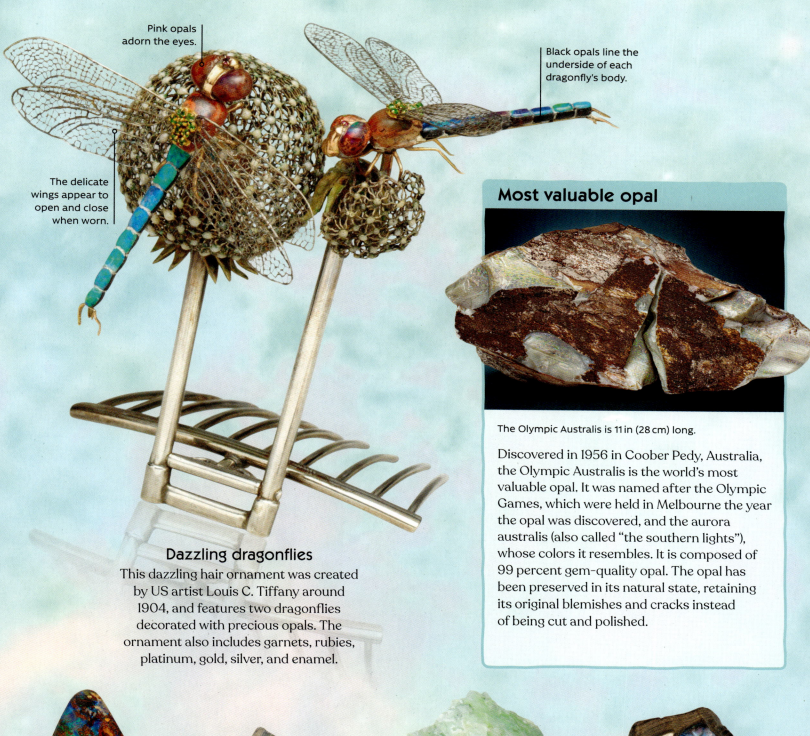

Pink opals adorn the eyes.

Black opals line the underside of each dragonfly's body.

The delicate wings appear to open and close when worn.

Dazzling dragonflies
This dazzling hair ornament was created by US artist Louis C. Tiffany around 1904, and features two dragonflies decorated with precious opals. The ornament also includes garnets, rubies, platinum, gold, silver, and enamel.

Most valuable opal

The Olympic Australis is 11 in (28 cm) long.

Discovered in 1956 in Coober Pedy, Australia, the Olympic Australis is the world's most valuable opal. It was named after the Olympic Games, which were held in Melbourne the year the opal was discovered, and the aurora australis (also called "the southern lights"), whose colors it resembles. It is composed of 99 percent gem-quality opal. The opal has been preserved in its natural state, retaining its original blemishes and cracks instead of being cut and polished.

Koroit
Opals from the Koroit area of Queensland, Australia, form inside sedimentary rocks rich in iron.

Fire
Fire opal is known for its red and yellow flame-like colors caused by inclusions of iron oxides.

Chrysopal
Chrysopal contains nickel, which gives it a light green color.

Opal in ironstone
This precious opal from Australia has formed in ironstone, still visible as a brown crust.

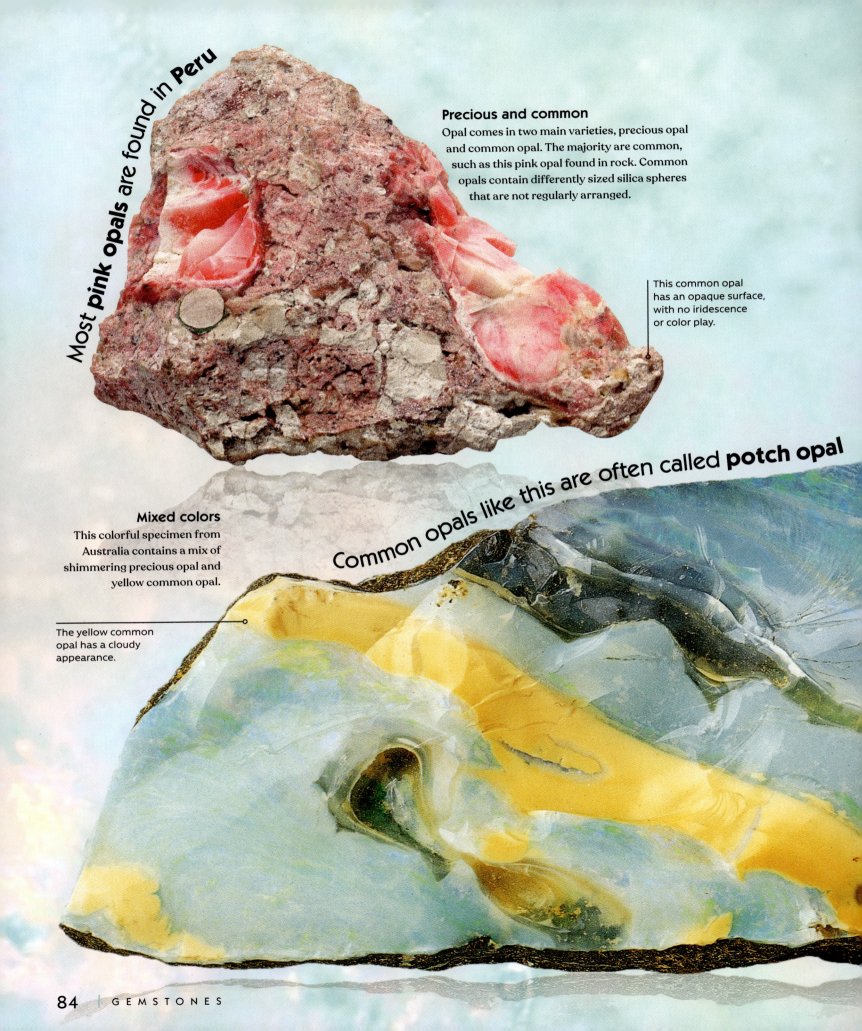

Most **pink opals are found in Peru**

Precious and common
Opal comes in two main varieties, precious opal and common opal. The majority are common, such as this pink opal found in rock. Common opals contain differently sized silica spheres that are not regularly arranged.

This common opal has an opaque surface, with no iridescence or color play.

Common opals like this are often called **potch opal**

Mixed colors
This colorful specimen from Australia contains a mix of shimmering precious opal and yellow common opal.

The yellow common opal has a cloudy appearance.

84 | GEMSTONES

How opals get their color

The colors in precious opal come from tiny silica spheres inside it. These spheres diffract (split) white light into the colors of the rainbow. The size and arrangement of the spheres determine which colors you see.

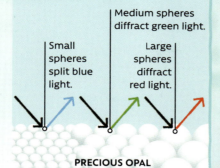

Small spheres split blue light.

Medium spheres diffract green light.

Large spheres diffract red light.

PRECIOUS OPAL

Siliceous sinter
These opals form in the water around hot springs and geysers.

Hydrophane
This opal's appearance is changed by water absorbed through tiny pores.

The ironstone in which this opal formed is still visible on the edge of the specimen.

Precious opals can take on a layered appearance, adding to the color play.

Opal reflects the light, much like glass does.

Matrix
When silica-rich water solidifies inside pores or as narrow veins in a rock, it is called matrix opal.

Pineapple
Opal has replaced and taken the shape of other crystals, giving it a pointy, pineapple-like look.

Hyalite
Sought-after for its purity, hyalite is a colorless common opal that usually shines under UV light.

Opal in boulders
This variety of precious opal is found in the seams of boulders.

The opal has broken in a smooth curve. This is called conchoidal fracture.

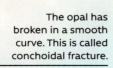

Fossil fill-in

Sometimes water rich in silica seeps into cavities inside rocks that contain fossils. If the geological conditions permit opal formation, this can result in an opalized fossil. Fine details of the surface—and sometimes the internal structures— of the fossil can be preserved in detail.

Opal has replaced the tooth of a plesiosaur, a marine reptile, alive at Lightning Ridge, Australia, c. 100 MYA.

OPAL | 85

Brooch
This art-nouveau brooch by Austrian goldsmith Ferdinand Hausner dates from around 1912. It depicts night-blooming lotus flowers on an enameled blue background reaching toward the moon. Thirteen more moonstone pendants hang from delicate gold chains.

The "moon" is made from a cabochon moonstone.

Natural fractures

Rough
In this specimen, flecks of minerals seem to make uncut moonstone glow from within.

Moonstone

This glistening mineral is a type of feldspar, a material composed mostly of aluminum, silicon, and oxygen.

Moonstone has a high potassium and sodium content. Layers of minerals inside the stone scatter and reflect light, giving its blue or white sheen, an effect that inspired the ancient Romans to believe it was made of solidified moonbeams. It is found in India, Australasia, East Africa, and Norway. Before it is polished, it often looks like frosted glass.

Moon god

Female archers sit behind Chandra. Their arrows of light drive away darkness.

In Hinduism, Chandra is the god of the moon. He is usually shown in a chariot, which is being drawn across the night sky—in some depictions by an antelope, and in others by 10 white horses or 10 white geese. He often holds a lotus flower and has a moon—or a crescent moon—carved from moonstone set into his forehead or the front of his crown. In recent times, India's lunar space mission has been named after Chandra.

Subtle peach colour

Refracted light appears to sparkle and glow.

Smooth finish
Moonstone is often polished into glassy dome cabochons.

Unusual color
An increased amount of aluminum gives this moonstone a peachy hue.

Shimmering stone
Moonstone is composed of feldspar layers, and each one reflects and diffuses light.

86 | GEMSTONES

Color-coded
The amber color of this uncut sunstone indicates it contains a high copper content.

Iron oxide "glows"
Flecks form into lines

Shining stone
Oligoclase moonstone like this is especially spangled, or "aventurine." Microcline sunstone is duller.

Opaque
Metallic inclusions create sunstone's sparkle and affect its transparency, ranging from translucent to opaque.

Flecks
Copper and iron-oxide flecks can make some sunstones appear deep amber.

Sunstone

A feldspar like moonstone, sunstone differs from its near-namesake by being more colorful.

Sunstone contains flecks of iron oxide and copper that catch and reflect light and give this gem its distinctive shimmer. The relative amounts of iron oxide and copper help determine its color. Sunstone has two main forms: oligoclase and microcline.

Faceting a gem enhances its varying shades.

Clean cut
Sunstone is usually cut into facets, unlike moonstone, which is polished smooth.

Sunstone is relatively soft and easy to cut into shapes.

Common color
Yellow-gold is a common sunstone color. Red and green are the rarest colors.

Dense mineral clusters

Inclusions
Many inclusions give this faceted oval sunstone a unique appearance.

MOONSTONE AND SUNSTONE

Labradorite

This gem is named after Labrador, a province in Canada, where it was first discovered in 1770.

Labradorite is a type of feldspar, which occurs in metamorphic and igneous rocks. It has its own unique iridescent sheen known as "labradorescence"—created by a series of thin layers of feldspar with different chemical compositions, which grow within the crystal as it cools. Though it was first found in Canada, labradorite is now mined all over the world, including in Madagascar, Finland, Russia, the US, and Mexico.

Rough stone
This rough specimen has labradorite's typical gemstone-grade blue color, with an uneven, splintery fracture.

Blue-and-green iridescence

Iridescence
The multicolored sheen on the broken surface of this specimen is a good example of labradorescence.

Iridescent skies

Labradorescence has inspired many legends. Some Inuit from Canada tell a tale of a hunter who saw light trapped inside a rock. He pierced it with his spear, sending some to the sky to become the northern lights, and leaving some to become labradorescence.

The northern lights are swirling patterns of colorful light.

88 | GEMSTONES

Uncut specimen
This rough labradorite specimen displays blue, gold, and green labradorescence, with a glassy luster.

Fractures criss-cross the surface of the stone.

Cut slab
Dazzling flashes of blue illuminate the surface of this cut specimen.

Yellow-and-bronze iridescence

The term "labradorescence" was first used in 1924

Spectrolite
Labradorite from Finland is known as spectrolite. This example has a gray-silver surface, with labradorescence on some areas.

LABRADORITE | 89

Lapis lazuli

There are few blues as vibrant as lapis lazuli, a precious stone prized for thousands of years.

Lapis lazuli is a metamorphic rock. Its vivid blue hue comes from the mineral lazurite, though the rock often contains other minerals, including white calcite and pyrite (also known as fool's gold). Lapis lazuli powder has been used as a medicine and as the pigment for blue colors in paint. It was also turned into eye shadow and worn by the Egyptian queen Cleopatra, among others.

Starry sky
Lapis lazuli is sometimes flecked with tiny flakes of pyrite, giving the impression of a night sky.

White calcite
The presence of the mineral calcite can reduce the value and appeal of a piece of lapis lazuli.

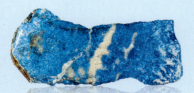

Chilean blue
Chile has some of the biggest deposits of lapis lazuli, which is the country's national gemstone.

Polished
Lapis lazuli is often sanded and polished to add shine to the stone's surface.

Top quality
The finest lapis lazuli is deep blue with violet tones, and few other minerals.

The deep blue of the mineral lazurite is caused by the element sulfur.

The other minerals aside from lazurite that make up lapis lazuli rock can appear as flecks, streaks, or solid pieces.

This **death mask** is among the **most famous** artifacts to survive from **ancient Egypt**

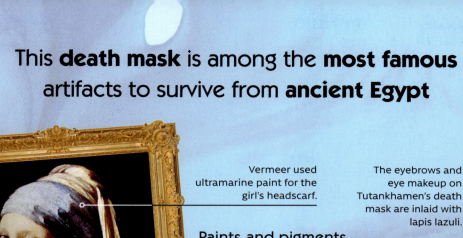

Vermeer used ultramarine paint for the girl's headscarf.

The eyebrows and eye makeup on Tutankhamen's death mask are inlaid with lapis lazuli.

Paints and pigments
Ultramarine paint has been on artists' palettes for hundreds of years. To create it, lapis lazuli was ground into a fine powder, added to a solution that included wax and oil, and strained through a cloth. The Dutch artist Johannes Vermeer applied ultramarine to several areas of his famous 1665 painting *Girl with a Pearl Earring*.

The Silk Road
Lapis lazuli was mined in Afghanistan from around 7000 BCE. It was one of the items traded along the Silk Road, an ancient route that connected China in the East to Europe in the West.

Trade flowed through cities along the route.

Easy to shape
Though expensive, lapis lazuli was used in ancient jewelery because it was easy to carve and shape.

The body of this winged scarab pectoral (breast plate) found in the tomb of King Tutankhamen is made from lapis lazuli.

Lapis lazuli means "blue stone" in Persian

Sumerian beads
This lapis lazuli and gold necklace dates from c. 2150 BCE and was found in a grave in Sumeria (modern-day Iraq).

Jadeite
In its purest form, jadeite is white, but additional minerals can alter its color.

Mutton-fat
White jades with yellow markings—known as "mutton-fat" jades—were sought after in ancient China and India's Mughal Empire.

Jade

"Gold has a value; jade is invaluable," **according to an ancient Chinese saying.**

The term "jade" really describes two different minerals: jadeite and nephrite. Jade has long been treasured by cultures around the world, especially in the Americas and East Asia. It is extremely tough and durable, and requires great skill to work into tools and beautiful objects. It is said that a Chinese king offered 15 cities to another king in exchange for a single jade carving.

Nephrite
In its rough state, nephrite is recognizable thanks to its fibrous, splintery texture and greasy green hues.

Shaping jade

In ancient China, jade was used to fashion burial suits for royal members of the Han dynasty. The tomb of Dou Wan, the wife of a Han prince, contained a burial suit made of 2,160 jade plaques.

The jade plaques completely sealed the body and were thought to confer immortality to her soul.

Working with jade
An artisan works on a piece of jade jewelry in Myanmar (Burma).

Gold thread was used to fit the jade plaques together.

92 | GEMSTONES

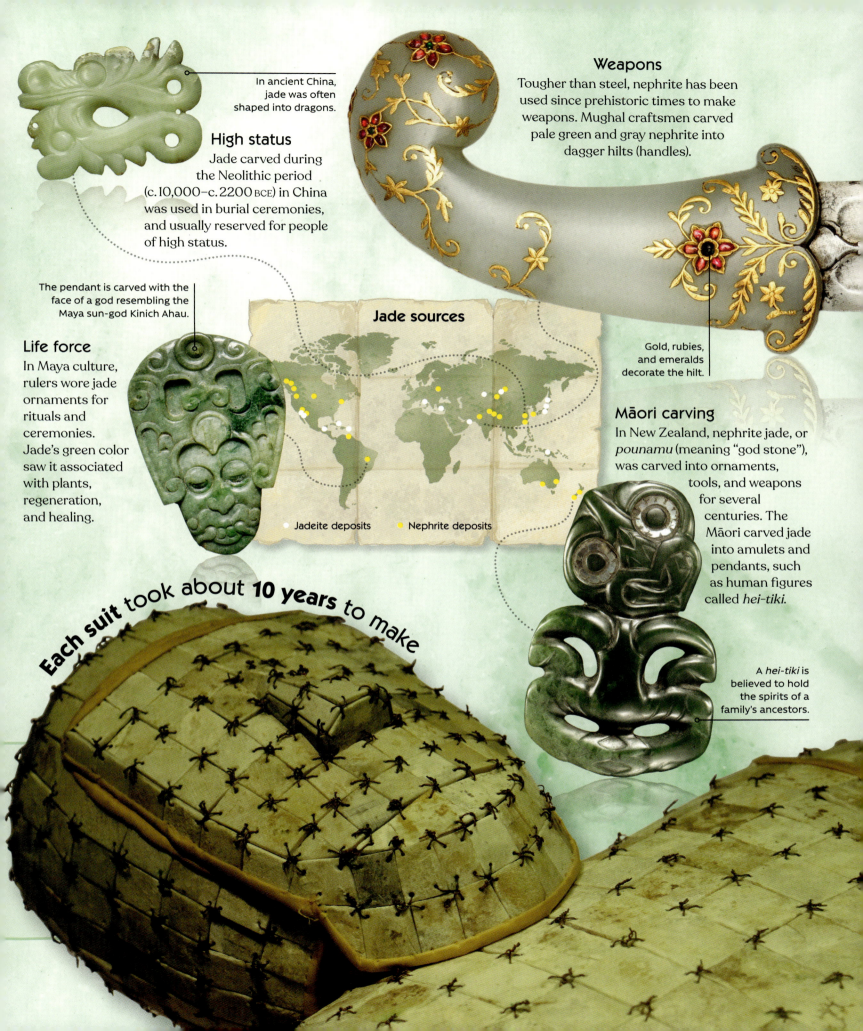

In ancient China, jade was often shaped into dragons.

High status
Jade carved during the Neolithic period (c.10,000–c.2200 BCE) in China was used in burial ceremonies, and usually reserved for people of high status.

Weapons
Tougher than steel, nephrite has been used since prehistoric times to make weapons. Mughal craftsmen carved pale green and gray nephrite into dagger hilts (handles).

The pendant is carved with the face of a god resembling the Maya sun-god Kinich Ahau.

Life force
In Maya culture, rulers wore jade ornaments for rituals and ceremonies. Jade's green color saw it associated with plants, regeneration, and healing.

Jade sources

- Jadeite deposits
- Nephrite deposits

Gold, rubies, and emeralds decorate the hilt.

Māori carving
In New Zealand, nephrite jade, or *pounamu* (meaning "god stone"), was carved into ornaments, tools, and weapons for several centuries. The Māori carved jade into amulets and pendants, such as human figures called *hei-tiki*.

A *hei-tiki* is believed to hold the spirits of a family's ancestors.

Each suit took about **10 years** to make

Mottled
The uneven, mottled look of this piece of jadeite is a result of inclusions in the stone.

Imperial
Imperial jade, a dark green variety, is rich in the element chromium.

Polished nephrite
Nephrite is often smooth, as a result either of polishing or of water flowing over it in a river.

Lilac
Lilac is one of the rarest colors associated with jade.

Jadeite stone
Vivid green jadeite stones such as this one have been used throughout history for carvings and jewelery.

Lavender jade
This purple-colored stone is only found in the Bursa province of Türkiye.

Red
In Chinese tradition, red jade rendered homage to the south— different colors were associated with points on a compass.

Rough
The splintery, uneven fractures on this rocky sample are typical of jadeite.

Its base colors range from gray-purple to rich, deep purple, with various mottling.

Yellow
Iron traces in jade can result in vivid yellow hues.

94 | GEMSTONES

Teysky jade
This rare variety of jade is only known from a mineral deposit in Khakassia, Russia.

Trees and pavilions

This nephrite boulder dates from the Qing dynasty, during the reign of the Qianlong Emperor (r.1735–1796), who was an enthusiastic collector of elaborate engraved objects. It depicts a mountainous landscape with pine trees and temples.

The boulder shows a route upward through mountain temples—probably a journey to the afterlife.

*Chinese philosopher Confucius said jade had **11 virtues**, including **loyalty** and **faith***

The Jade Emperor

In Chinese mythology, the Jade Emperor is often described as a human who, through his kindness, wisdom, and intelligence, became immortal (able to live forever), and later, a god. In the Daoist religion, the Jade Emperor lives in a palace made from jade and is the ruler of heaven and everything below it.

This painting is a typical depiction of the Jade Emperor in long, flowing clothes, surrounded by his court.

JADE | 95

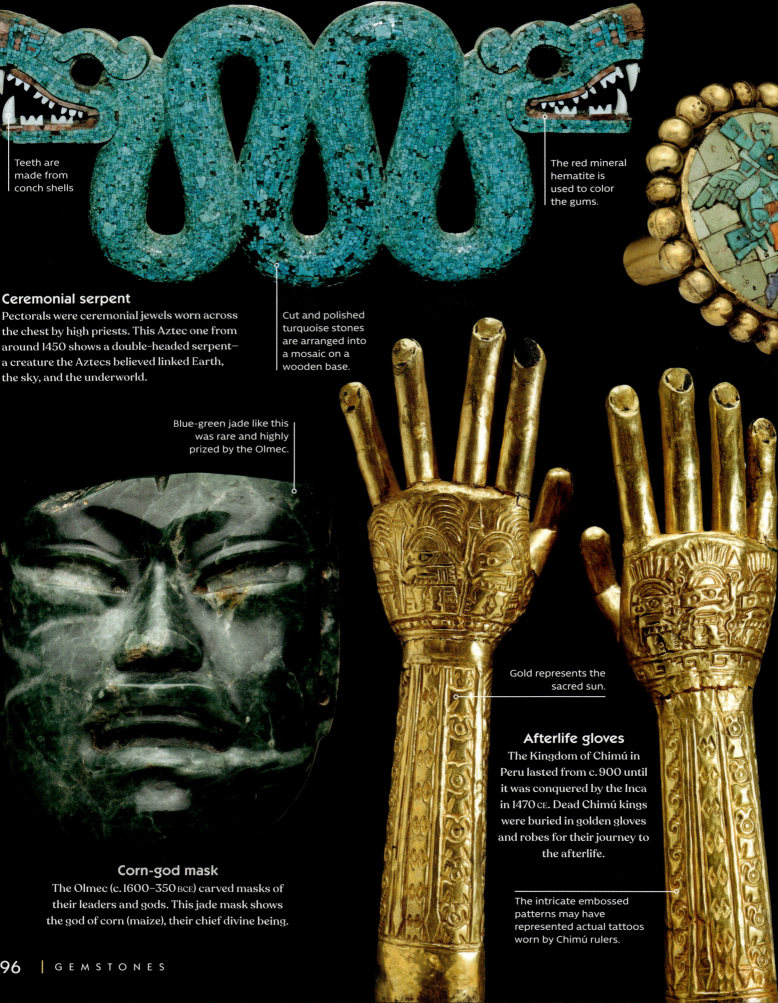

Teeth are made from conch shells

The red mineral hematite is used to color the gums.

Ceremonial serpent
Pectorals were ceremonial jewels worn across the chest by high priests. This Aztec one from around 1450 shows a double-headed serpent—a creature the Aztecs believed linked Earth, the sky, and the underworld.

Cut and polished turquoise stones are arranged into a mosaic on a wooden base.

Blue-green jade like this was rare and highly prized by the Olmec.

Gold represents the sacred sun.

Afterlife gloves
The Kingdom of Chimú in Peru lasted from c. 900 until it was conquered by the Inca in 1470 CE. Dead Chimú kings were buried in golden gloves and robes for their journey to the afterlife.

Corn-god mask
The Olmec (c. 1600–350 BCE) carved masks of their leaders and gods. This jade mask shows the god of corn (maize), their chief divine being.

The intricate embossed patterns may have represented actual tattoos worn by Chimú rulers.

96 | GEMSTONES

Ear ornaments

This pair of ornamental ear pieces was assembled from gold, shell, turquoise, and other blue-green stones by Moche artists, who lived in modern-day Peru between 400–700 CE. Many of the materials were imported. The cost and difficulty of this probably means that these ear ornaments were worn by a high-status person.

The figure is probably an owl in human form.

The figure is probably the civilization's founder god, Naymlap.

Each figure is shown running while holding a small bag.

Inlaid turquoise symbolizes sacred water and the sky.

TREASURES OF
the Americas

Central America (Mesoamerica) and South America were home to many powerful empires before European colonizers arrived in 1492. Civilizations including the Olmec, Maya, Sicán, Aztec, and Moche worshipped the sun, the moon, and other gods. They celebrated and honored their deities with highly decorated artifacts, often in gold, and studded with turquoise and other precious stones.

Sacrificial knife

Priests from Peru's Sicán culture (750–1350 CE) used this gold *tumi* (ceremonial knife) for human and animal sacrifices. *Tumis* were precious objects and Sicán leaders were often buried with them.

Sharp blade

Tourmaline

Tourmaline's chemistry is "more like a medieval doctor's prescription than the making of a respectable mineral," according to 19th-century English writer John Ruskin.

With a complex recipe involving many ingredients, tourmaline comes in more than 100 color varieties—more than any other gemstone. There are more than 30 varieties of tourmaline, including dravite, elbaite, and rubellite. Most tourmalines form in igneous rocks, but they can also be found inside gravel dumped by rivers.

Tourmaline typically forms prisms (elongated crystals) with a triangular cross-section.

Copper and manganese traces give Paraíba tourmaline its blue color.

Dravite
This magnesium-and-sodium-rich variety was first found near Slovenia's Drava River.

Elbaite
Rich in lithium and sodium, this specimen has multiple colors within a single crystal.

Paraíba
This is the rarest and most expensive tourmaline. It was first found in Paraíba, Brazil.

Double tourmaline
This green tourmaline bottle, made during the Chinese Qing dynasty (1644–1911), has a pink tourmaline stopper.

The carved detail depicts an old man carrying a baby.

An empress's favorite

A large pink tourmaline adorns the center of the empress's headdress.

The Chinese Dowager Empress Cixi loved tourmaline so much that China became the main importer of this gemstone during her reign in the 19th century. She was particularly fond of pink tourmaline from southern California—so much so that she helped start a boom (flourishing) of the tourmaline industry there in the early 1900s.

Ancient ornament
This brown and yellow tourmaline has been carved to show the profile of Greek king Alexander the Great (356–323 BCE). It represents the oldest known use of tourmaline as an ornament.

Alexander is shown wearing the ram-shaped horns of the god Zeus Ammon.

Multicolored
This pink and orange crystal contains different chemicals at either end.

Rubellite
One of the most admired varieties of tourmaline for its striking colors, this rubellite is raspberry pink.

Schrol
Iron gives this tourmaline variety a dark brown and black color.

Long crystals
This specimen had space and time to grow into a mass of many elongated, spiky crystals.

TOURMALINE | 99

Burst of color
The interplay of chemicals produces bursts of color in tourmaline. This example has a pink center, with hues changing to colorless, blue, and green toward its edges.

Crystals with many color bands are called particolored.

A long search
Brazilian gemstone prospector Heitor Dimas Barbosa spent five long years digging in Brazil's northeastern mountains, convinced that a new gemstone was waiting to be found. He was proved right in 1989 when he discovered a variety of tourmaline called Paraíba.

Barbosa with Paraíba tourmaline

Circular crystal inclusions of rubellite

Rubellite in rock
This specimen shows crystals of rubellite growing inside a mass of blue minerals on rock.

100 | GEMSTONES

Zones of color

Tourmaline crystals can display several colors in one specimen. This color zoning happens when the chemicals around the crystal change as it is forming. This can lead to triangular growth zones in the crystal, or colors changing throughout the crystal. The effect can be enhanced when the gemstone is polished and cut into thin slices.

This tourmaline displays stunning color zoning.

The color zoning in this specimen is triangular in outline.

Watermelon
This specimen—with a pink center and a dark green outer edge—is called watermelon tourmaline, because its appearance resembles the fruit.

The crystals end in rounded fan shapes.

The red and pale pink crystals have a glassy look and sheen.

Mushroom shape
Tourmaline can grow into complex crystal shapes, such as this mushroomlike mass of rubellite crystals.

TOURMALINE | 101

Emerald

This is one of the most cherished precious stones, thanks to its rarity and bright green color.

Emeralds are a variety of the mineral beryl. Their vivid color is created by the presence of small amounts of chromium and vanadium. Emeralds come in a wide spectrum of greens—some are opaque, but the finest of all are almost transparent. The ancient Egyptians were the first people known to have mined emeralds, 4,000 years ago, and these sparkling green stones have been prized as gemstones ever since.

Each crystal has six sides.

Emerald crystals embedded in quartz

Six-sided structure
When emeralds form naturally, their crystals grow in a hexagonal (six-sided) formation.

Rough
Rough emeralds are found in veins of calcite or quartz, which run through shale or limestone.

Little sparkle
Before they are cut, emeralds have a rich green color but little sparkle.

In rock matrix
Many people appreciate the natural, rough look of emeralds that have formed within a rock matrix.

Crown of the Andes
Many emeralds have been found in Colombia, and they have often been used to decorate religious objects. This gold crown was made in honor of Mary, the mother of Jesus. It features nearly 450 cut emeralds.

The cross is inlaid with 10 emeralds, carefully positioned end-to-end.

Clusters of emeralds are arranged in flowerlike shapes.

Byzantine beauty
The Byzantines developed their own unique artistic style featuring polished and shaped emeralds. This 6th–7th-century Byzantine necklace is made of gold, with circular emerald inlays and beads.

Each triangle has 10 gold cells, which are inlaid with emeralds.

Around the world
The exquisite Mughal Emerald is the world's largest inscribed emerald. It was mined in Colombia and shipped to Spain before being sold in India. The emerald was then carved around 1695, during the reign of Aurangzeb, the last great emperor of the Mughals, though it was probably owned by a noble or official in the empire rather than the emperor.

A Shia prayer is carved into the emerald.

The emerald is 2 in (5.2 cm) long.

Trapiche
Sometimes emerald crystals grow in a rare six-pointed shape called a trapiche.

Polished bead
This polished bead was found in northern Egypt and comes from ancient Roman times.

EMERALD | 103

Crystals
Here, aquamarine crystals are seen among fragments of rock.

The crystals contain traces of silver and other minerals.

Red beryl

Known from only Utah and New Mexico, red beryl is many times more valuable than gold. It is the rarest of all beryl gemstones, and rarer even than diamond. Around one red beryl is found for every 150,000 diamonds.

Beryl

Beautiful beryl comes in several colors. The sea-blue variety is called aquamarine, and was once thought to bring good luck to sailors.

Beryl is a mineral prized for its stunning range of colors, which include green emeralds as well as aquamarine. Beryl is a tough crystal. It can form in granites, pegmatites, volcanic rocks, and metamorphic rocks, such as schists. It also forms in gaps within rocks, developing inside cavities or veins.

Aquamarine
The sea-blue color of aquamarine is produced by traces of iron in the crystals.

Cluster
These six-sided aquamarine crystals have formed in a cluster. They have blue-green hues.

Sky-blue crystals
This mass of aquamarine crystals has striations (a series of ridges) on its surfaces and a glassy shine.

Portrait of an empress

A portrait of an empress has been carved into this beryl. Empress Julia Domna was the wife of ancient Roman emperor Septimius Severus. This likeness of her was made in around 200 CE.

A figure carved into a gem is called an intaglio.

Space mirror

Beryl is named after the element beryllium— a metal that is part of the gem's chemical composition. Beryllium is tough, resilient, and light, making it ideal for use in space. The 18 mirrors of the James Webb Space Telescope (JWST) are made of gold-plated beryllium. They reflect light from far-away galaxies onto recording devices.

An artist's impression of the JWST in space

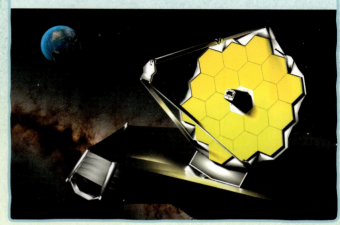

The gem is 13¾ in (35 cm) tall.

This six-sided crystal has a pyramid-shaped top.

Striations can be seen on the crystal's faces.

Flat-faced crystal
This beryl crystal has flat, well-defined faces. It is still attached to the rock it grew in.

Dom Pedro aquamarine
This obelisk-shaped gem from Brazil is the world's largest known aquamarine.

Heliodor
Traces of iron can also produce yellow hues, creating a variety of beryl called heliodor.

Green
Minas Gerais in Brazil is an important source of beryl, such as this flat-topped green beryl.

BERYL | 105

Uvarovite
Uvarovite is often found in the form of tiny green crystals and is one of the rarest of all garnets.

The crystals are often dodecahedral, which means that they have 12 sides.

Grossular
Less dense than other types of garnet, grossular can be found in most colors, from yellow to green, peach, and black.

Garnet

This tough, crystalline stone is found in a variety of colors and has uses ranging from decorative to commercial.

Garnet is an overall term for a range of silicates—minerals combined with metal oxides. These include red almandine, purple rhodolite, and green tsavorite. As well as being gemstones, garnets are used for industrial purposes, such as in sandpaper and water purification systems.

Tiny miners

In the US Southwest, ants often bring garnets to the surface when digging tunnels in the ground. From there, the stones are washed down by rainwater, collecting in large numbers at the bottom of the anthill.

Ants can typically carry between 10 and 50 times their body weight.

Garnets were polished and shaped before being inserted into the metal grid.

Pearls and diamonds ring the bright red garnet at the center of this piece.

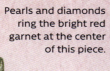

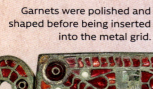

Seeds and stones

In Greek mythology, Hades, the god of the underworld, tricked Persephone into eating pomegranate seeds, binding her to his realm for part of the year. As a result, garnets are often associated with pomegranate seeds, which they resemble in shape, color, and size. The word "garnet" originates from the Latin *granatus*, meaning "seed."

Bejeweled belt buckle
Red garnets decorate this 6th-century Spanish belt buckle, inlaid in bronze and accompanied by colored glass. This style of decoration, known as cloisonné, was popular with the Visigoths who ruled Spain and Portugal around 400–700.

Love and friendship
Red garnet is often associated with love and friendship. This makes it ideal for jewelery designed to be given as a present, such as this gold pendant from 1870.

Eagle fibula
The Visigoths viewed garnet as a stone of status and protection, and used it to decorate many items of clothing. A fibula (brooch fastener), such as this garnet-encrusted eagle, would have been used to secure a cloak.

*This exquisite brooch may have been **owned by a queen***

Red garnet is placed within a gold-plated bronze design.

Garnet is set within beaded gold wire.

Kingston brooch
Large red garnet stones form part of the decoration of the 7th-century Kingston brooch. It was found in the grave of a wealthy Anglo-Saxon woman, and also features gold, shell, blue glass, and pearl.

The garnet is named after Spessart in Germany, where it was first found

Spessartine
The orange color of spessartine reflects large amounts of the mineral manganese in this rare garnet. It is found as crystals in varying structures, including dodecahedral and euhedral (when the crystal develops its natural geometric shape).

Garnet crystals are hard, measuring 7–7.5 on the Mohs scale.

Twelve or 24 faces are typical for an almandine crystal.

Uvarovite
The intense, bright green color of uvarovite comes from the presence of chromium in its makeup.

Andradite
Andradite is found in colors including brown, green, and black. This black example is pictured alongside the green mineral diopside.

Titanium andradite
Melanite or titanium andradite contains more titanium than iron.

108 | GEMSTONES

In rock matrix
This specimen features raspberry-red garnets in a rock matrix comes from Sierra de las Cruces, Mexico.

Rhodolite
A hybrid of the garnets pyrope and almandine, the rare rhodolite is typically a pretty shade of rose pink, which makes it sought-after for jewelery.

Panning for garnets

Like gold, garnets can be "panned" to separate them from river sediment. The Panhandle National Forest in Idaho is renowned for garnet panning. There, visitors can sift through river-bed gravel to try to pick out garnets ranging in size from a grain of sand to a golf ball.

Garnets have a dense composition similar to that of gold.

Almandine
The deep red of the almandine garnet comes from the presence of iron.

GARNET

Buried treasure

Found buried in a field in England in 2009, the Staffordshire hoard is made up of more than 4,000 pieces of gold and silver inlaid with garnet that once decorated the weapons, armor, and battle dress of 7th-century Anglo-Saxon warriors. We don't know why many show signs of having being pulled off of swords and helmets, nor why they were deliberately buried.

Buried treasure

Found buried in a field in England in 2009, the Staffordshire hoard is made up of more than 4,000 pieces of gold and silver inlaid with garnet that once decorated the weapons, armor, and battle dress of 7th-century Anglo-Saxon warriors. We don't know why many show signs of having being pulled off of swords and helmets, nor why they were deliberately buried.

Zircon

Smooth, shiny surface

The word zircon is from Persian, *zargoon*, meaning "golden." However, the stone comes in a range of colors other than gold.

Some zircon colors are bright and fiery, including yellows, oranges, and reds. It can also be green or colorless, or have areas of different colors within a single crystal. Zircon can be found as pebbles in river beds or as crystals in rocks. In medieval Europe, it was thought to grant a peaceful night's sleep to those who owned it.

Smooth, rounded pebble

Pebble
This green zircon pebble is from Sri Lanka. Some zircons contain so much uranium and thorium that radioactivity breaks down the crystal structure, causing changes to color, refraction, and density.

Rectangular crystal with pyramid-shaped end

Rough
Zircon crystals are often orange or brown in their natural state. They can be heated to turn them blue or white.

Ancient minerals
Zircon crystals from Western Australia are the oldest-known minerals on Earth. They are 4.4 billion years old, which means they formed just 160 million years after Earth itself.

These ancient crystals are tiny, visible only through a microscope.

Yellow
Pure zircon is transparent. Yellow zircon gets its color from traces of iron.

Orange
The presence of uranium or thorium can make a zircon orange.

112 | GEMSTONES

Changing color
Some zircons have color zonation: the color shifts across the stone. This may be caused by conditions when the crystal was growing, or possibly by heat or radiation after it formed.

Color shift from orange to green

Refraction
Colorless zircon shines brightly, which means it is sometimes confused with diamond. However, the two gemstones have different properties, such as their refraction: how light travels through them.

Colorless zircon

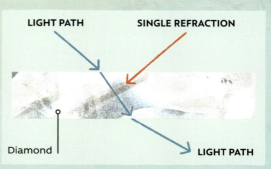

Single refraction
When a ray of light passes through a diamond it is refracted (it bends) but does not split—it is refracted just once. Diamond, garnet, and spinel are singly refractive.

Zircon crystal

In matrix
This red zircon is shown growing in its rock matrix.

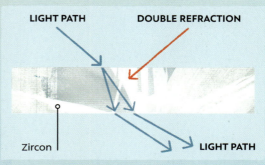

Double refraction
When entering a zircon, a single ray of light is split into two rays, which travel at different speeds and in different directions. This telltale double refraction is an easy way for gemologists to tell zircons and diamonds apart.

Red
Large amounts of uranium or thorium will produce a red zircon.

Fiery
Zircon comes in a wide variety of orange, red, and yellow flame colors.

Green
Eventually, a zircon containing radioactive uranium will turn green.

Topaz

It was once thought that all yellow gems were topaz, and topaz only came in yellow, but we now know that neither is true.

Topaz comes in a rainbow of color options. The stone is usually very clear, with no visible inclusions, and its hardness and shiny appearance make it a popular choice for jewelery. Topaz is a silicate gem, containing aluminum and fluorine. It is typically found inside and around the igneous rocks granite and pegmatite, as well as in river gravels.

Mega crystals

Most topaz crystals are quite small, but some grow to be gigantic. The world's largest known topaz crystal, found in Minas Gerais, Brazil, weighs 596 lb (271 kg)—as heavy as a male alligator. Topaz mega-gems have been found in Brazil for decades.

This yellow topaz mega-gem was also found in Minas Gerais, Brazil.

The end of the crystal is pyramid-shaped.

Lines called striations are common on the surface of a topaz.

Rough
Blue-green hues like this one often occur when there are imperfections in a topaz crystal.

Brazilian
This long, red-brown crystal is from Brazil. It is transparent, making it ideal for use in jewelery.

Brilliant cut
The layered facets of this colorless topaz reflect and direct light beautifully, enhancing its brilliance and sparkle.

Ostro Stone
Weighing 4 lb 7 oz (2 kg), the Ostro Stone is the world's largest blue gemstone. Its vivid color was created by treating it with heat and radiation.

Topaz is very hard, which makes it resistant to scratches

Orange
This translucent orange crystal is from Siberia, Russia, an area famous for its large topaz crystals.

Topaz crystals have grown on top of larger quartz crystals.

Imperial
Imperial topaz has golden, reddish-brown hues. It was highly prized by the Russian czars (emperors).

Pink
Pink is the most rare and valuable color of all topaz. It contains chromium, and tends to form long crystals.

TOPAZ | 115

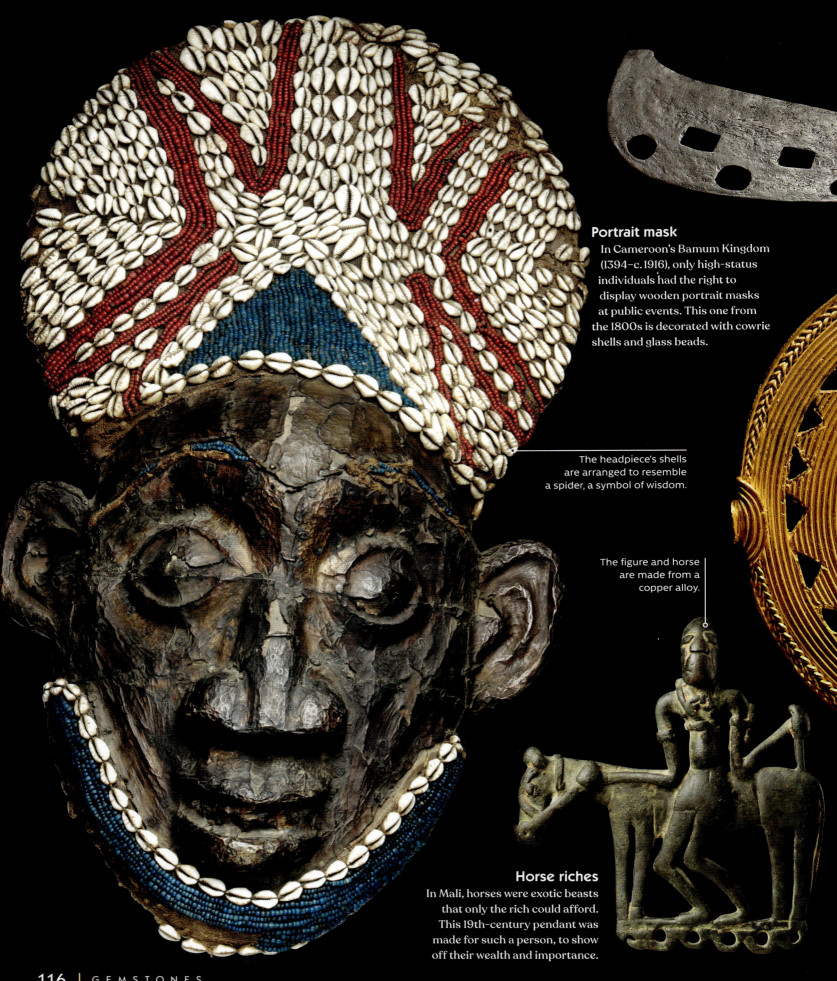

Portrait mask
In Cameroon's Bamum Kingdom (1394–c. 1916), only high-status individuals had the right to display wooden portrait masks at public events. This one from the 1800s is decorated with cowrie shells and glass beads.

The headpiece's shells are arranged to resemble a spider, a symbol of wisdom.

The figure and horse are made from a copper alloy.

Horse riches
In Mali, horses were exotic beasts that only the rich could afford. This 19th-century pendant was made for such a person, to show off their wealth and importance.

116 | GEMSTONES

Decorative sword
This ceremonial sword dates from the end of Ghana's Asante Empire (c. 1700–1901). Its iron blade is fixed to a golden hilt (handle) decorated with geometric designs and human faces.

The handle is made of wood, coated in gold leaf.

Detailed patterns have been worked into the gold.

TREASURES OF West Africa

The states of West Africa had been established and thriving for thousands of years before European colonists arrived in the area. The wealth that funded the beautiful artifacts shown here was based on trade in the region's abundant natural resources: gold, silver, bronze, and cloth.

The elephant's body is hollow, so that it could be filled with incense, which slowly wafted out from it.

Sacred elephant
Silver sculptures such as this one were made for the shrines of the rulers of the Kingdom of Dahomey (c. 1600–1904) in modern-day Benin. Elephants represented strength, long life, and memory.

Important people only
This gold armor was made by the Asante people in the early 20th century. It is a pectoral, a piece designed to be worn across the chest. Only high-ranking members of the royal court wore them, including chiefs and officials who served the king.

TREASURES OF WEST AFRICA | 117

Other treasures

The following treasures all have different origins. Some, such as pearls and amber, are formed by living things. Glassy obsidian is created when volcanic lava cools rapidly, while marble and sandstone are rocks produced by Earth that are prized for their beauty and usefulness.

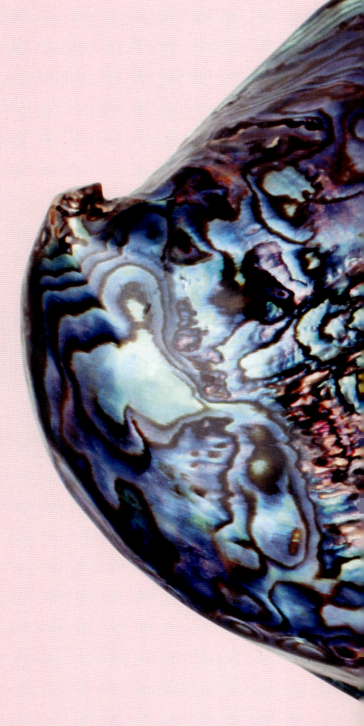

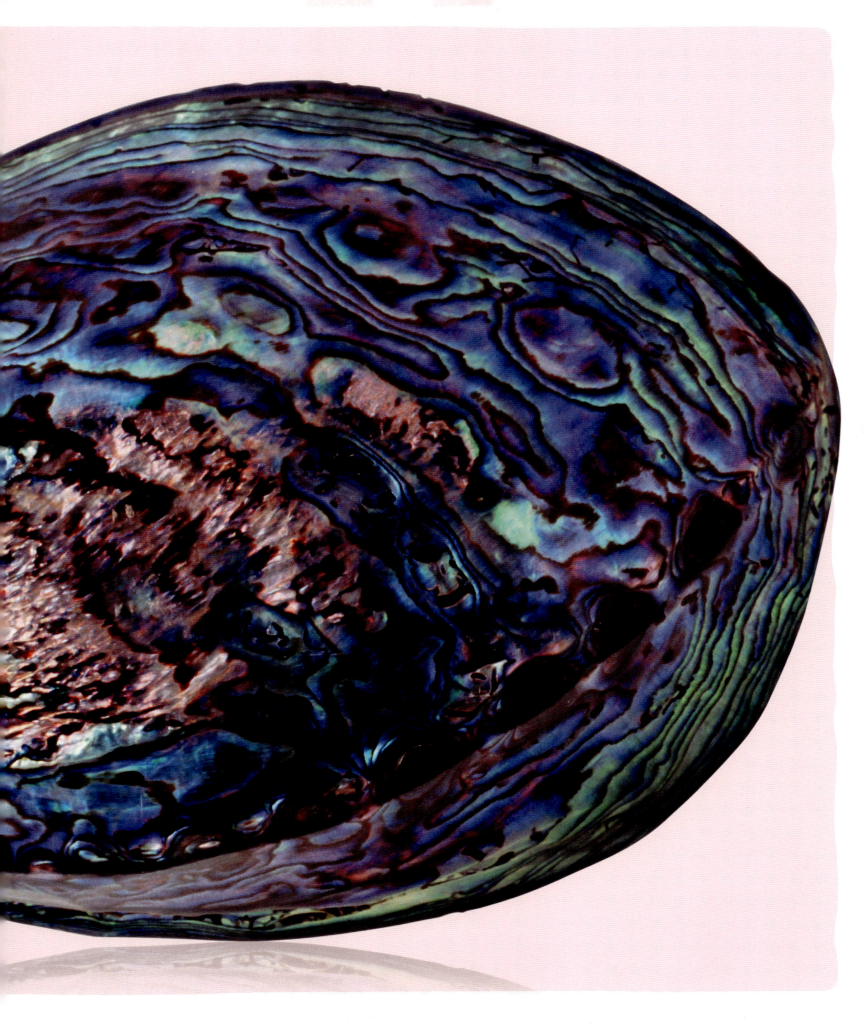

The inside of the shell is covered in nacre (mother-of-pearl), which is the same substance that pearls are made of.

The pearl develops inside the soft body of the oyster.

Pearl oyster
The pearl oyster is the most common pearl-producing saltwater mollusk. It creates the finest-quality gems.

The pearls in each pattern are uniform in size.

Pearl

Shimmering pearls are the only gemss that are made by living creatures. Their beautiful sheen has made them highly desired since ancient times.

Pearls are created by saltwater and freshwater mollusks: soft-bodied creatures such as oysters and mussels, that live inside shells. Some pearls grow naturally but most are cultured, which means that their development is triggered by human involvement.

120 | OTHER TREASURES

Caddoan necklace
This necklace features freshwater pearls from the Mississippi Delta region. It was made between 1200 and 1400, by the Caddoan people.

Insect brooch
A beautiful gray-green pearl forms the body of the insect in this brooch, made by a US jeweler in the 1890s. It reflects a trend at the time for jewelery modeled on the natural world.

Pearl sources

Top pearl producers

Perfectly round pearls like this one are the most expensive of all.

Royal crown
The Russian royal family used pearls in their crowns, tiaras, and orbs. This 17th-century crown is encrusted with hundreds of pearls.

How a pearl forms

A pearl begins when a foreign object such as a grain of sand enters an oyster. The mollusk builds layers of a material called nacre (mother-of-pearl) around the sand to protect itself.

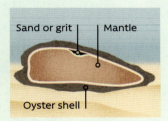

Sand or grit | Mantle
Oyster shell

1. Sand enters oyster
Sometimes, a stray piece of sand or grit will find its way inside an oyster shell and get stuck there.

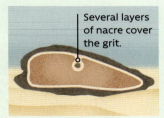

Several layers of nacre cover the grit.

2. A nacre coat
To protect itself, the oyster coats the grit with nacre, creating a "pearl sac."

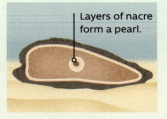

Layers of nacre form a pearl.

3. A new pearl
Over time, the tiny piece of grit is coated in many layers of nacre, becoming a solid pearl.

PEARL | 121

A high-quality pearl shows a vibrant and iridescent sheen.

Classic
The ideal pearl is perfectly round, with no marks on its smooth, shimmering surface.

Cultured
These are made when humans add foreign objects to oysters, to kick start pearl development.

Black
The nacre produced by Tahitian black-lipped oysters contains a pigment that creates black-colored pearls.

Pink baroque
Irregularly shaped pearls are known as "baroque" pearls. They come in a variety of colors.

Freshwater
The most common pearls are found in freshwater mollusks—mainly pearl mussels—from China, the US, and Japan.

Queen conch
The rare pearls produced by the queen conch sea snail are not made of nacre, but of a mineral called aragonite.

Massive pearl

The largest natural pearl ever found is known as the Giga Pearl. This colossal baroque blister pearl weighs 61 lb (27.65 kg), which is about as heavy as a Labrador Retriever. It grew on the inside of the shell of a giant clam and is now displayed as part of an artwork, alongside a golden sculpture of an octopus.

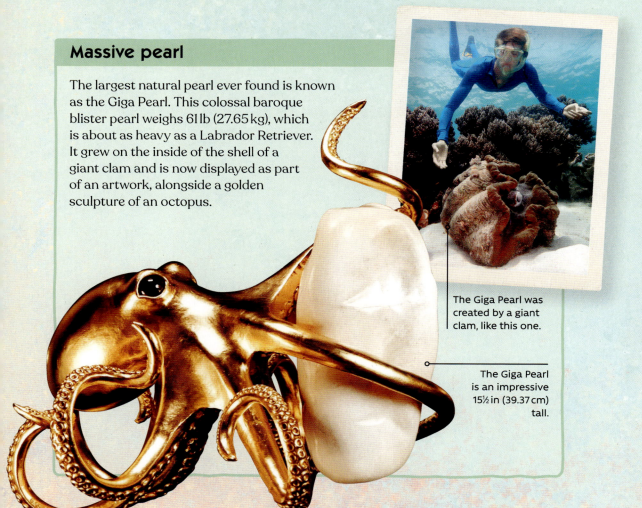

The Giga Pearl was created by a giant clam, like this one.

The Giga Pearl is an impressive 15½ in (39.37 cm) tall.

Fossil
Pearls can become fossilized. These examples are up to 200 million years old.

Nacre attaches the blister pearls to the shell.

This **baroque pearl** has an **iridescent sheen** of **green, purple, and yellow**

Blister
Pearls that grow on the inside of a shell are known as blister pearls. They often have one flat edge.

Pearl divers

On the South Korean island of Jeju, women have been trained to dive for pearl oysters and other shellfish for hundreds of years. They are known as *haenyeo*, and they can hold their breath for more than two minutes at a time, helping them to increase their catch.

Some *haenyeo* keep diving well into their 80s.

Freshwater baroque
Baroque pearls have uneven shapes, ideal for unique pieces of jewelery.

Tyrian purple

The most expensive clothing color of the ancient world was probably Tyrian purple, named after the Phoenician city of Tyre (in modern-day Lebanon) where it was traditionally processed. This natural dye was painstakingly extracted from the mucus of the spiny murex sea snail. Only emperors, kings, and important officials were allowed to wear clothes dyed in Tyrian purple.

The sharp spines of the murex sea snail made harvesting the dye difficult.

Tyrian purple

Wentletrap
This sea snail has a striking spiral shape and is often white. It is popular for making jewelery.

Delicate ribs run along the length of the shell.

Shell

People have always admired the beauty of shells—we have worn them throughout history.

Shells form from a hard layer of calcium carbonate—a mineral that some sea creatures make to protect themselves. When the animal dies, its shell does not decay. Some shells are simple, while others display incredibly intricate shapes, patterns, and colors. Shells are often used to create ornaments and jewelery, but they have less obvious uses, including as currency and a source of vibrant clothing dyes.

The shiny material inside is called nacre, or mother-of-pearl.

Nautilus
The shiny inner coating of the nautilus shell is often used to make jewelery.

Green tree snail
This shell became so popular with jewelers that the green tree snail is now endangered.

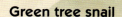

Cowrie shells

Harvested in the Indian and Pacific oceans, cowrie sea snail shells have been used as money since the 13th century BCE. Cowries first appeared as currency in China, followed by Africa, Asia, and Oceania. They were useful as money because they are small, easy to harvest, slow to wear away, and similar in size and shape.

Cowrie shells are usually about 1¼ in (3 cm) long.

The ridges along the shell's opening are called denticules.

This figure is probably a tiger.

Deer race away from the oncoming hunters.

Shell art
Created around 300–100 BCE, this shell is the oldest surviving image of people and animals in Chinese history. Known as "The Hunt," it shows archers in a four-horse chariot (top) and a two-horse chariot (bottom), hunting animals. The scene has been painted on the inside of a clam shell.

Nature's trumpet
On the Fijian island of Viti Levu in the South Pacific, conch shells were used as trumpets to send signals. Finger holes bored close to the shell's opening allowed the player to change the note being played.

Glory-of-the-seas cone
Its rarity, shape, and beautiful coloring make this the most collectible seashell of all.

SHELL | 125

Fossilized beauty

In the right circumstances, the shells of marine creatures can form stunning natural treasures, such as this fossilized ammonite shell. In this case, mineral crystals (likely quartz) have formed within the shell's cavities, transforming its color and making it even more eye-catching.

Mother-of-pearl

The iridescent shine of mother-of-pearl is like nothing else in the natural world. It is made from nacre, the same material as pearls.

Mother-of-pearl is found inside the shells of the same types of shellfish that can make pearls. It has a glittering, silvery surface, which can feature a wide range of colors, including whites, pinks, and greens. The composition of mother-of-pearl is unique: nacre is made of a mineral, aragonite, and a protein, conchiolin. These are arranged in interlocking "tiles," which make it strong and flexible.

Nacreous shell
A thin layer of nacre covers the inside of this shell. The colors appear to change, depending on which angle it is seen from.

Abalone
Abalone shells show darker colors than most mother-of-pearl shells.

Abalone interior
Inside an abalone shell there is a thin layer of mother-of-pearl, with distinctive green tones.

Turban
Mother-of-pearl can appear on the outside of shells, as well as inside. This is a turban shell, belonging to a tropical species of sea snail.

Nacre patterns swirl across the outside of the shell.

128 | OTHER TREASURES

Inside the coyote's jaws

This 1,000-year-old artwork is a very elaborate jar lid, which was made by the Toltec people of modern-day Mexico. Decorated with dozens of pieces of mother-of-pearl, it features the head of a coyote, with a warrior's face between its jaws.

The coyote's teeth are made from animal bone.

Carefully carved pieces of mother-of-pearl interlock across the surface of the piece.

A warrior's head emerges from inside the coyote's mouth.

The base of the piece is made from clay.

MOTHER-OF-PEARL | 129

Tsimshian masks

These striking masks were created by the Tsimshian—an Indigenous people of the Pacific Northwest coast of North America. Both masks show a bird-human hybrid and are crafted from wood, with abalone shell mother-of-pearl highlights. They are used in special ceremonies and to enact stories to help keep Tsimshian traditions alive.

Sea-snail shells are placed in alternating directions.

Ancient skills
The Palawa people of Tasmania, Australia, have been making necklaces from shells for at least 2,600 years. These necklaces are worn as jewelery and also used as currency.

The mosaics show the inner mother-of-pearl layer of the nautilus shell, which is shiny and iridescent.

TREASURES OF
Oceania

Oceania is a vast area, centered around the North and South Pacific oceans. It includes Australia, New Zealand, and thousands of tiny islands in Melanesia, Micronesia, and Polynesia. Oceania's art and culture are incredibly diverse, often featuring themes of gods, spirits, nature, and ancestor worship.

Woven shield
This shield was made in the Solomon Islands in the 19th century. It is made from rattan (woven palm stems) inlaid with nautilus-shell mosaics.

Sacred shell

Engraved oyster shells, known as riji, have a central place in the culture of First Australians in northwestern Australia. They are designed to be worn, and are given to mark the transition of their owner from boy to man, and to mark the wearer's status. They have been traded over vast distances for centuries.

Fine obsidian has been skillfully carved, creating a sharp cutting edge.

The sacred patterns stand out against the mother-of-pearl of the shell.

Obsidian knife

This 19th-century knife is from the Admiralty Islands, north of New Guinea. It is called a gudom, and has a carved wooden handle with a blade made of obsidian.

Hei matau designs range from very simple to highly ornate.

Ocher has been rubbed into the grooves to highlight the patterns.

Good luck

A *hei matau* is a symbolic fish hook, usually made from pounamu (jade). *Hei matau* are given by the Māori people of New Zealand to bestow good luck and safety when traveling across water.

TREASURES OF OCEANIA | 133

Whitby
Jet often washes up on the beach at Whitby Bay, UK. It is the best-quality jet.

Polished
When polished, jet has a deep black, matte, velvetlike shine.

Cut
Polishing and faceting jet can produce a shiny, mirrorlike finish.

Heat and compression
Jet formed from dead trees that fell into the sea. The dead trees were covered by sediment, then heated by Earth and compressed over millions of years.

Jet

Throwing dice
These jet dice were made in 14th–15th-century Britain. They have been kept in a rough, unpolished state that shows the jet's layers and dark brown color.

The dots, or "pips," have been scratched into the soft material.

This dark substance is the remains of trees that have turned into coal.

Jet is a mineraloid—a mineral-like substance that does not contain crystals. It usually forms from conifer trees, including monkey puzzles, which petrify (turn to stone) over long periods of time. Jet is quite rare. It is flexible and easy to carve into jewelery, ornaments, and statues.

Fine details have been carved into the jet.

Spanish statue
Jet has a striking color and is easily shaped. It is often used to make small but intricate figurines, such as chess pieces. This Spanish statue of St. James was made in Spain in around 1410.

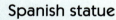

Rough
Layers of compression can be seen clearly on this freshly mined jet.

134 | OTHER TREASURES

Uncut wood
This specimen has not yet been cut into shape.

Tree growth rings are visible here.

How peanut wood formed

The worms feed off the wood.

1. Tunneling worms
Trees in ancient forests were buried and became waterlogged. Worms dug tunnels through the trees' wood.

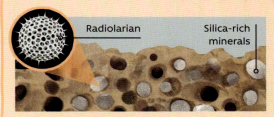

Radiolarian | Silica-rich minerals

2. Watery minerals
The tunnels filled up with silica-rich water, which contained the mineral skeletons of tiny marine creatures called radiolarians.

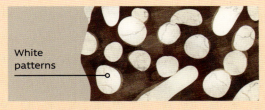

White patterns

3. Fossilization
As the minerals solidified, the wood was fossilized, preserving the worm holes as distinctive peanut-shaped patterns on a wood-colored stone.

Peanut wood

This little-known material is used to make valued and sought-after jewelery.

Found only in Western Australia, peanut wood is named after the nut-size markings that speckle its surface. These were caused by prehistoric worms boring holes into wood. The holes then filled up with dissolved white sediment from plankton shells as the timber fossilized on the ocean floor.

Polished
This example is pale, with long, white sediment streaks.

Round cabochon
A round cabochon cut highlights the "peanut" effect.

Elongated cabochon
A rectangular cabochon cut can accentuate longer markings.

JET AND PEANUT WOOD | 135

Amber

Yellow
Around two-thirds of all amber found is yellow.

Amber is tree sap that has been fossilized. It has a striking yellow-orange color and can contain other objects, such as insects.

It takes millions of years for amber to form. It begins as resin (sticky fluid), produced by certain trees. If those trees die and decay underground, pressure and time cause the resin to harden and turn into amber. If any tiny plants or animals get stuck in the resin, they may be preserved along with it, captured inside a piece of amber forever. Amber's translucent orange glow makes it popular for making jewelery and ornaments.

The clearer the amber, the more valuable it is as a gemstone.

Cloudy
Tiny air bubbles trapped in amber make it cloudy.

Green
Chlorophyll pigment from plants can make amber green.

Red
Amber can turn red if it reacts with oxygen in the air.

Dinosaur tail

This amber from Myanmar (Burma) contains the tail of a sparrow-size dinosaur. It is at least 100 million years old, and the dinosaur tail's feather-like structures are perfectly preserved inside the amber.

"Feathers" inside the amber

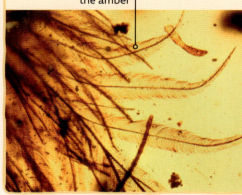

Prehistoric prison

This prehistoric fly got caught in sticky resin before it solidified, and is now encased in a piece of Baltic amber. Most of the world's amber is found in the Baltic countries (Estonia, Latvia, Lithuania), but not all of it contains insects.

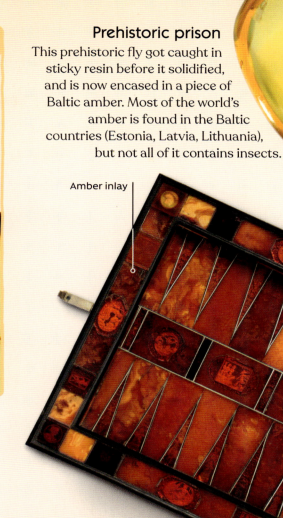

Amber inlay

An air bubble in the amber may be the insect's last breath.

Stealing peaches

Amber is relatively soft, which makes it easy to carve. This ancient Chinese amber carving depicts an old man stealing magical peaches.

The old man believes the peaches will extend his life.

Game time

This 17th-century folding backgammon and chess board is inlaid with amber. Amber has been used to decorate game boards for centuries.

Wood resin

All amber forms from the tree resin of certain conifer trees, including pines, spruces, and firs. Its purpose is to protect the tree: it is released to seal up wounds in the bark if the tree is damaged.

AMBER | 137

Eighth Wonder

The Amber Room in St. Petersburg, Russia, is often called the "Eighth Wonder of the World." More than six tons of carved amber—the same weight as an elephant—decorate the walls. Gold leaf and mosaics made from quartz, jade, and onyx add to the splendor. The room was completed in 2003, and was inspired by a similar room made in Germany in 1701 that was lost during WWII.

Coral

Corals are collections of tiny animals called polyps, which live together in huge undersea colonies.

Polyps have no bones. However, they excrete calcium carbonate, a mineral that forms hard exoskeletons around their bodies. When the polyps die, the skeletons remain, becoming the coral that jewelery and artifacts can be made from. Coral collection is now discouraged, because it harms coral reefs.

Danger, coral!

In June 1770, soon after first landing in Australia, English sailor James Cook accidentally ran his ship aground on the treacherously sharp coral of the Great Barrier Reef. HMS *Endeavour* and its crew survived, but since then more than 1,200 vessels have been sunk by the reef.

This 1886 illustration shows HMS *Endeavour* swaying after hitting the underwater reef.

Red
Highly sought-after red coral is only found in the Mediterranean and Adriatic seas.

Many corals form branchlike structures.

Polished red
Polishing can enhance coral's color. The red color seen here is created by organic pigments called carotenoids.

Black
The dark hue of black coral is created by a protein called conchiolin, which is similar to keratin, the substance found in animal horn and hair.

Blue
Iron salts dissolved in sea water can give coral this bright blue-green color.

The shaft is decorated with two colors of coral.

Enamel inlays surround the coral.

Nails unbroken
In China's imperial era, which ended in 1911, important men and women grew their fingernails long. This coral-decorated finger guard protected the wearer's nails from breaking.

The surface is soft enough for a detailed relief to be carved into it.

Gently does it
Coral can be brittle and difficult to work with. Jewels made from it are rarely faceted. It is easier to polish and then carve decorative designs into it, as was done with this cameo of a woman from Naples, Italy. Coral cameos were very popular in Italy in the 18th century.

A delicate rose
The rare and expensive angel skin coral in the center of this gold ring has been shaped into rose petals, which complement its pink color.

Coral carving of Medusa from the 1st or 2nd century BCE

A frightening gaze
In Greek mythology, a gaze from the monstrous gorgon Medusa turned anyone who looked at her to stone. After the hero Perseus beheaded her, Medusa's blood turned seaweed in a nearby river into red coral. As a result, the Greek word for coral is *gorgeia*, which means "gorgon" in English.

CORAL | 141

Obsidian

Both an igneous rock and a naturally occurring glass, obsidian has a unique origin and history.

Obsidian forms when the lava that spews out in a volcanic eruption cools rapidly. It is best known in its shiny black form, but can also contain rainbow- or snowflake-like patterns, which form when particular minerals or gases are present. Obsidian's hardness and attractive colors have made it a popular choice for jewelery, carvings, axes, and knives since ancient times.

Smoking Mirror

In the Aztec culture of ancient Mexico, polished, glassy obsidian mirrors were used to call on gods and ancestors. The Aztec god Tezcatlipoca is often shown carrying obsidian mirrors, and is also known as "Smoking Mirror."

Aztec obsidian mirror

Mirror attached to Tezcatlipoca

This specimen has a brittle, splintery appearance.

Rough
This example shows how shiny and glassy obsidian is, even in its rough natural state.

142 | OTHER TREASURES

Snowflake cat

This cat figurine is carved from a type of obsidian that contains pale, snowflake-like crystals of the mineral cristobalite. The cat has been polished, giving it a glass-like, shiny finish.

Cristobalite snowflakes

The edge of an obsidian blade is sharper than a steel knife.

Neolithic arrowhead

Obsidian's edges can be razor-sharp. This makes it very useful: it has been shaped into cutting tools and weapons, such as this arrowhead, since the Neolithic period (c. 10,000–c. 2200 BCE). Obsidian was traded over vast distances by different civilizations around the world.

Striking patterns can form when rainbow obsidian is polished.

Rainbow

Rainbow-like patterns can appear in obsidian when tiny amounts of minerals or gas bubbles are present and arranged in specific patterns.

Lava glass

Not every volcanic eruption produces obsidian. It forms when lava solidifies so quickly that there is no time for crystals to grow, creating a glassy, smooth rock.

Obsidian near an active volcano in Iceland.

Cristobalite crystals

Conchoidal lines on the surface

Mottled

Pale crystals of cristobalite, a type of quartz, give this obsidian a mottled, spotty appearance.

Mahogany

Iron can form orange patterns in obsidian, creating what is sometimes called "mahogany obsidian."

Conchoidal fracture

When obsidian breaks, it fractures into curved, smooth, conchoidal surfaces.

Silver sheen

Minerals present in obsidian as it forms can cause it to become pale, with a silver sheen.

OBSIDIAN | 143

Sandstone

After shale, sandstone is the second most common sedimentary rock on Earth.

Sandstone begins as the sand that gives it its name: tiny grains of weathered rock. These grains build up into masses and then get squashed together into new rock. Sandstone can be different colors depending on which minerals are present. It is mostly used in building and for carving.

Sandstone city
Petra in Jordan was carved into sandstone cliffs by the Nabataean civilization, around the 3rd century BCE. It is nicknamed the "rose red city," due to the rusty red color of the rocks, created by the presence of iron oxide.

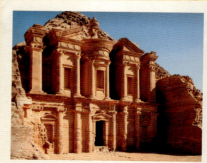

The Monastery building in Petra

Grainy
Here, the individual grains that form the sandstone are visible.

Hindu god
Sandstone is a soft rock with a smooth and even texture, which makes it perfect for use in decorative carving. This is a very finely detailed 10th–11th-century carving of the Hindu god Vishnu. An array of animals, patterns, and objects have been worked into the rock.

Smaller figures, including his wives and attendants, surround Vishnu.

Layered
Layers form when sediments pile up underwater.

Pieces of shell can be seen in the rock.

Embedded skeletons
Despite being exposed to enormous pressures and salty water, some shells and marine animal skeletons stay intact in limestone. Valuable fossils can be extracted by dissolving the stone in vinegar.

Sponge
These rounded shapes are the fossilized remains of ancient sponges.

Coral
Here, coral has been fossilized, becoming the mineral magnesium carbonate.

Limestone

This sedimentary rock is mainly made from the mineral calcite, and often contains shells and bones.

It forms when coral, shells, and dead marine life are squashed together over millions of years, and their remains fossilize into calcite and other minerals. This creates a white or creamy stone that is used for building and as an additive in paints and plastics.

Limestone pools
The milky white terraces at Pamukkale, Türkiye, are made of limestone. They were created by calcite-rich spring water flowing down the hillside over 600,000 years, coating it in a fine limestone crust.

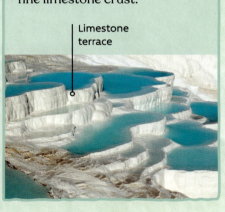

Limestone terrace

Crinoid
This limestone contains the fossilized remains of sea creatures called crinoids.

The pyramids of Giza
The pyramids at Giza, Egypt, were built from locally sourced nummulitic limestone. Nummulites are the marine creatures whose fossilized shells are found in this stone. The Great Pyramid alone contains 2.3 million limestone blocks.

Only part of the fine outer layer remains.

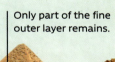

Ammonite
These ammonite shells were fossilized around 200 MYA.

145

Colors and stripes

You'd be forgiven for thinking that this image of the Zhangye National Geopark in China has been altered or painted in some way. In reality, layers of sandstone and minerals that have built up over millions of years, combined with tectonic activity and weathering, have created the unique angled stripes and vibrant colors that can be seen today.

Carrara
Top-quality Italian Carrara marble has a fine grain and gray veining.

Connemara
The green hue of this Irish marble is from the mineral serpentine.

Breccia
Italian breccia marble includes fragments of rock called brecicles.

Red
Red marble occurs when iron oxide is present in the stone.

Marble

Marble typically contains hairline cracks within the stone.

Widely used by sculptors and architects, marble is an elegant variety of stone.

Marble is composed of limestone that has been recrystallized after being exposed to extreme heat or pressure deep underground. It is smooth, durable, and comes in many beautiful colors—qualities that have made it a great choice for use in homes, monuments, and grand palaces.

Parthenon Sculptures

Once part of the 5th-century BCE Temple of Athena (the Parthenon) in Athens, Greece, the Parthenon Sculptures include panels carved in marble.

Marble panels show battles, gods, and scenes from Greek mythology.

The fine-grained marble came from Mount Pentelicus, near Athens.

148 OTHER TREASURES

Changing colors

For the Mughals who completed the Taj Mahal in Agra, India, in 1648, the brilliant white of the marble used to construct the mausoleum represented divine purity. The strong stone was also chosen for its changing light through the day, from pink to white to gold.

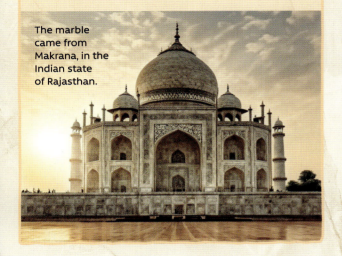

The marble came from Makrana, in the Indian state of Rajasthan.

The marble was carved with chisels and files, then smoothed down with pumice stones and leather.

Michelangelo's *David*

Carrara marble was used by Italian artist Michelangelo to create his famous *David* sculpture in 1504. The artist visited the Carrara quarries in Tuscany, Italy, to choose the finest marble for his work.

Memorial stone

Marble's durability, finish, and ability to be easily carved has led to its use as memorials since ancient Greek times. This 12th-century Iranian gravestone is intricately inscribed with Arabic script.

Passages from the Qur'an are carved into the marble.

Mining marble

Large machines—including excavators, saws, and trucks—look like toys in this huge marble quarry in Türkiye. Marble was once extracted by blasting it with explosives, but today, distinct blocks are cut from the mother rock using diamond-wire saws and drills. The blocks are then loaded onto trucks and transported to a processing plant, where they are turned into cut and polished products for customers.

These "mountain-shaped fittings" are designed to hang a strap from, so the weapon can be carried.

TREASURES OF
Japan

Flowers and animals appear often in Japanese art, reflecting a deep appreciation for nature that has always been central to Japanese culture. For more than 1,000 years, Japanese artisans have preserved traditions and celebrated religious rituals through the creation of beautiful objects made of gold, copper, mother-of-pearl, and turquoise.

Gold coin
Japan's shōgun rulers introduced the solid gold koban coin in 1601. It was valued at one koku of rice, which was enough to feed one person for a whole year.

The stamps give important information, including how much the coin is worth.

Nara mirror
This mirror is from the Nara Period in the 8th century, when Nara was Japan's capital. The front features highly polished bronze. The back is decorated with floral patterns in mother-of-pearl, turquoise, red amber, and green snail shell.

152 | OTHER TREASURES

Ceremonial sword
Only high-ranking warriors were allowed to carry ceremonial swords. This 12th-century example features gold and silver carvings of chrysanthemums and other flowers.

The scabbard is decorated with long-tailed birds, inlaid with mother-of-pearl.

Nacre (mother-of-pearl) is a glimmering substance that builds up on the inside of oyster shells.

Dirt and some tarnishing of the statue suggests that this object was buried for a long time.

The helmet is mounted with the crest of the Daté family, daimyo (lords) of Sendai.

Buddhist attendant
This 6th-century gold-plated bronze figure is Seishi Bosatsu. He is a legendary character: an attendant to Amida, the chief god in Pure Land, the most popular Japanese form of Buddhism.

Golden armor
This suit of armor is made of copper covered in a thin layer of gold. It was made in the 17th century for a daimyo (lord). Daimyo were powerful landowners in ancient Japan. They were skilled warriors and controlled armies of samurai.

TREASURES OF JAPAN | 153

Glossary

alloy A metal made up of two or more metals.

allochromatic Meaning "other-colored," it describes colorless gems that are colored by impurities.

amorphous Without a regular internal atomic structure or external shape.

asterism The star effect seen in some gems, such as rubies and sapphires.

atom The smallest unit of a chemical element.

basalt Earth's most common volcanic rock, usually made of solidified lava.

bedrock The layer of rock below the soil.

brilliance How bright a gemstone is, which depends on how much light it reflects back to the person looking at it.

brilliant cut The most popular cut for diamonds and many other stones. The standard brilliant has 57 facets, or 58 if the gem is cut with a flat face at the base.

cabochon A type of cut in which a gemstone is cut into a round or oval shape with a plain, domed upper surface.

calcite A colorless or white mineral found in sedimentary and metamorphic rocks.

cameo A design that has been cut into layered stone or shell, with the background material cut away.

carat The standard measure of weight for gemstones. One carat equals 0.007 oz (0.2 g).

cleavage The way in which a crystal splits apart along certain well-defined planes, according to its internal structure.

composition The fixed or well-defined chemical makeup of a mineral.

crust The outer layer of Earth above the mantle, including both continental crust and oceanic crust.

crystal A solid structure with its atoms arranged in a particular repeating three-dimensional pattern.

crystalline Having an orderly and repetitive structure of atoms within a solid.

cushion A square cut with rounded sides and corners.

cut The shaping of a gemstone by grinding and polishing, or the shape of the final gem (e.g. brilliant cut).

deposition The laying down of material such as sand and gravel in new locations, usually by wind, water, or ice.

deposits An area with lots of minerals or rocks formed as a result of a natural process.

dichroic A term that is used to describe a gem that appears to be two different colors when viewed from different directions.

diffraction The splitting of white light into its constituent colors.

durability The capacity to last for a long time without wearing out.

element A chemical substance that cannot be broken down further.

enamel A colorful glassy finish melted onto the surface of pottery or metal.

erosion The removal or wearing down of weathered pieces of rock into sediment by water, wind, or ice.

evaporation When a liquid changes to a gas.

extrusive rock Rock formed from lava that flowed onto Earth's surface or was ejected in an ash cloud.

face A flat surface on a crystal.

facet A flat surface of a gemstone, formed when it is cut.

faceting Creating flat surfaces on gems by cutting and polishing them.

fancy cut A gem cut into an unconventional shape, such as a heart.

feldspar A common type of silicate mineral found in igneous rock.

fire In gemstones, a term used for dispersed light. A gem with strong fire sparkles with the colors of the rainbow.

fluorescence The glow of some gems under ultraviolet light, caused by impurities in their crystal structure.

fossil A trace of past life that has been preserved in a rock or mineral such as amber.

gemologist A scientist who studies and evaluates gemstones.

gemstone A beautiful, high-quality, hard mineral, which is valued for its color and rarity. Gems usually have a near-perfect, or unique, crystal shape.

geode An open space in a rock that has mineral crystals.

gold leaf A very thin foil made of hammered gold and applied to objects for decoration.

granite One of the main igneous rocks found in continental crust.

granular Having grains, or being in the form of grains.

groundwater Water present beneath Earth's surface in the rocks and soil.

habit The shape in which a crystal naturally occurs.

hardness Of a mineral, the extent to which it can resist scratching or abrasion.

hydrothermal Description of something that formed in hot waters originating below Earth's surface.

idiochromatic Describes minerals whose color is part of their chemical composition.

igneous A type of rock formed by the cooling of liquid magma to lava, either deep inside Earth or at the surface.

igneous intrusion A body of igneous rock that formed when magma cooled and solidified underground.

inclusions Material (usually a mineral) trapped within another mineral.

intaglio A design in which the subject is cut lower than the background; the reverse of a cameo.

intergrown When two or more minerals grow together and interlock.

intrusive rock Igneous rock that has solidified below Earth's surface, cooling slowly enough to allow larger crystals to form. A body of intrusive igneous rock is called an igneous intrusion.

iridescence A rainbow-like play of colors on the surface of a mineral.

lapidary A skilled cutter of gemstones who is able to obtain the best optical effect.

lava Magma that has erupted at Earth's surface.

lodestone A piece of magnetite, a naturally occurring magnetic iron oxide.

luster The shine of a gem, caused by reflected light.

magma Hot, molten rock created in the mantle.

mantle The middle, thickest layer of Earth, lying above the outer core, and made mostly of hot, dense rock.

massive A term used to describe minerals that have no particular shape.

matrix The rock in which a gem is found. Also known as groundmass, host rock, or parent rock.

metamorphic A type of rock formed when heat and pressure change the structure of a rock that already exists.

meteorite A rock from space that has fallen to Earth's surface without completely burning up.

mica Shiny silicate mineral with a layered structure, found as tiny scales in granite and other rocks, or as crystals.

microcrystalline A mineral structure in which crystals are too small to be seen with the naked eye.

mineral A naturally occurring solid with a distinctive crystal structure and a specific chemical composition.

mineraloid A mineral-like substance with many, but not all, of the properties of a mineral.

mixed cut A type of cut that combines the facets used in brilliant and step cuts.

Mohs scale Scale showing the relative hardness of one mineral when compared to another.

molten Object, such as a rock, that is turned to liquid by heating.

mounting The jewelery piece that a gem is, or gems are, set into. Also called a setting.

nacre A substance made of calcium carbonate that creates the sheen on pearls and some seashells as they reflect light. Also known as mother-of-pearl.

native element A chemical element that occurs in a pure state in nature, such as gold.

opalescence A milky blue form of iridescence.

opaque A material that does not let light pass through.

ore A rock or a mineral from which a valuable metal or element can be obtained.

organic gem A material that is made by animals or plants.

oxidize To combine chemically with oxygen.

particolored Single crystals that are made up of different colors.

pegmatite Igneous rocks that may contain very large crystals, formed from the very last water-rich magma to crystallize.

pendeloque cut A lozenge-shaped cut, often used for flawed gems.

piezoelectricity A property of quartz crystals. Pressure on a crystal creates positive and negative charges.

pleochroic Describes a gemstone that looks as if it is two or more different colors when viewed from different directions.

porous Able to absorb water or other fluids.

precious metal A valuable metal, such as gold or silver.

prismatic A term that describes crystals in which parallel rectangular faces form prisms.

property A characteristic of a mineral, crystal, or gemstone, such as its color.

pyroclastic rock The fragments of rock, pumice, and solid lava that may explode from a volcano.

radiation Energy released by tiny particles or waves.

refraction When light changes direction, or bends, as it passes from one medium to another.

rock A combination of mineral particles, mixed up together.

rough The natural state of a rock or crystal.

sandstone A rock made of sand grains cemented together by other minerals.

sediment Weathered grains of rock that have been, or are being, transported by natural processes.

sedimentary A type of rock formed by the weathering, erosion, and transporting of sediments that are deposited in an ocean or lake, where they are cemented together and buried to form new rocks.

silica A hard mineral made from silicon and oxygen, which is the basis for Earth's most common minerals. Things containing silica are called silicates.

silt Fine particles carried by water.

stalactite A deposit of calcium carbonate hanging from the roof of a cave.

stalagmite A deposit of calcium carbonate rising from the floor of a cave.

step cut A rectangular or square-cut gemstone cut with several facets, parallel to the edges of the stone. It is generally used for colored stones.

striation Parallel lines, grooves, or scratches in a mineral.

sulfide Mix of sulfur with one other chemical element.

sulfur A yellow element, common in rocks and often erupted from volcanoes.

synthetic gemstone An artificial gemstone that has a chemical composition and properties similar to the natural gem from which it is copied.

tectonic plate One of many large, platelike pieces of Earth's crust, which move independently of one another over a very long period of time.

translucent A material that allows some light to pass through it.

transparent A material that allows light to pass through it.

ultraviolet (UV) light Type of light invisible to humans that makes some minerals glow.

vein A narrow crack in a rock that works as a pathway for fluids, including molten rock or mineral-rich water; veins can become filled with solid minerals over time.

Index

Page numbers in **bold** refer to main entries.

A

abalone shells 128
African civilizations 25, 33, **116–117**
African onyx 70
agate **68–71**, 72–73
Agua Nueva agate 68
alloys 33
almandine 106, 109
amber **136–137**, 138–139
amethyst **60–61**
ametrine 61
ammonite shells 126–127, 145
amulets 69, 93
ancient civilizations 18–19
　Africa 25, 33, **116–117**
　Aztec Empire 24, 55, 96–97, 142
　India 26–27, 46–47, 86, 149
　Japan 152–153
　Mesoamerica 50, 96–97
　Oceania 132–133
　Rome 64, 66–67, 103, 105
　see also China; Egypt, ancient; Greece; ancient
andradite 108
angel skin coral 141
Anglo-Saxons 107, 110–111
ants 106
anyolite 44
Apache agate 70
aquamarine 104–105
aragonite 122, 128
armor 111, 117, 153
Asante Empire 117
Aztec Empire 24, 55, 96–97, 142
azurite **51**

B

bamboo agate 71
Bamum Kingdom 116
Banded Iron Formation (BIF) 78–79
Barbosa, Heitor Dimas 100
baroque pearls 122, 123

basalt 8
beauty 14
beliefs 18
　see also religions
beryl 102, **104–105**
black coral 141
black diamond 34
black opal 82
black pearls 122
black spinel 49
blister pearls 122, 123
blue agate 70, 71
blue beryl (aquamarine) 104–105
blue coral 141
blue sapphire 40
blue spinel 49
botryoidal form 15, 52, 65
bowls 33, 50, 69
bracelets 31, 66
Brazilian agate 68
Brazilian amethyst 60
Brazilian topaz 115
breccia marble 148
brilliant cuts 17, 34, 115
bronze 80, 107
Bronze Age 69
brooches 86, 107, 121
brown copper 32
brown diamond 35
brown tourmaline 99
Buddhism 46, 47, 153
bullion 25
burial treasure 23, 66, 96
　Anglo-Saxon 110–111
　Chinese 80, 92, 93
　Egyptian 53, 91
busts 29, 30
Byzantine Empire 103

C

cables 33
cabochon 17, 135
Caddoan people 121
calcite 90, 145
calcium carbonate 124, 140
cameos 17, 65, 69, 141
carats 17
carbonado 34

carbonates 11
carnelian 63, 66
Carrara marble 148, 149
carved gems 17
Central America 96–97
chalcedony **62–65**, 68, 74
chalcopyrite 32
chandeliers 58–59
chevron zonation 60
Chilean lapis lazuli 90
Chimú Kingdom 96
China **80–81**, 99, 125, 141
　jade 18, 92, 93
　Silk Road 91
chrysopal 83
chrysoprase 64
citrine 57
Cixi, Empress Dowager 99
clarity 17
cleavage 13
coal 134
coins 19, 22, 29, 152
color 14, 17, 85
color zoning 101, 113
colorless quartz 54
colorless sapphire 41
conch shells 125
conchoidal fracture 13, 64, 143
Connemara marble 148
Coober Pedy, Australia 82, 83
Cook, James 140
copper **32–33**, 50, 51, 52, 87
coral **140–141**, 145
corundum 40, 42
cowrie shells 125
Coyamito agate 68
crinoids 145
crowns 19, 23, 81, 103
　Russian 49, 121
　tiaras 43
crystal balls 55
crystal chandeliers 58–59
crystals 9, 15, 16
　amethyst 61
　beryl 104–105
　chalcedony 64
　copper 32
　emerald 102

quartz 55
ruby 42, 44
silver 28
spinel 48
topaz 114
tourmaline 99
zircon 112
Cullinan Diamond 35
cultured pearls 122
cuts, gemstones 16–17, 61, 71, 115

D

daggers 46, 93
Dahomey, Kingdom of 117
Delhi Purple Sapphire 61
dendritic form 15
diamond 13, **34–35**, 36–37, 54
dinosaurs 137
Dom Pedro aquamarine 105
dravite 98
durability 14
dyes 51, 91, 124

E

ear ornaments 97
Egypt, ancient **30–31**, 50, 53, 145
　jasper 74, 75
　lapis lazuli 90, 91
elbaite 98
elements see native elements
emerald **102–103**, 104
Ethiopian opal 82
even fracture 13

F

fancy cuts 17
feldspar 86, 87, 88
fiery zircon 113
fire agate 70
fire opal 83
First Australians 132–133
fool's gold (pyrite) 22, 55, 90
fossils 85, 123, 135, 145
　amber 9, 36–137
　ammonite shells 126–127, 145
fractures 13, 143
freshwater pearls 120, 122, 123

156 | INDEX

G

games 75, 134, 137
garnet **106-109**, 110-111
gems, organic *see* organic gems
gemstones **14-17**, 52-53
    agate 68-71, 72-73
    amethyst 60-61
    azurite 51
    beryl 102, 104-105
    chalcedony 62-65, 68, 74
    emerald 102-103, 104
    garnet 106-109, 110-111
    jade 18, 80, 92-95
    jasper 30, 74-77, 78-79
    labradorite 88-89
    lapis lazuli 31, 90-91
    malachite 51, 52-53
    moonstone 86, 87
    opal 82-85
    quartz 54-57, 58-59
    ruby 15, 42-45
    sapphire 40-41, 42, 61
    spinel 48-49
    sunstone 87
    topaz 114-115
    tourmaline 57, 98-101
    turquoise 50, 80
    zircon 112-113
    see also minerals
geodes 56, 57, 60, 64
Giga Pearl 122
glory-of-the-seas cones 125
gneiss 8
gold 9, **22-25**, 26-27
Greece, ancient **66-67**, 99, 148
    mythology 87, 107, 141
green amber 136
green amethyst 61
green beryl 105
green jasper 76
green tree snail 124
green zircon 112, 113
grossular 106

H

hackly fracture 13
halides 11
hardness 12-13

health 19, 28, 90
heliodor 105
Herkimer diamonds 54
Hinduism 44, 46-47, 86, 144
Hirst, Damien 36-37
horses 80, 116
hyalite 85
hydrophane opal 85

I

Ife people 33
igneous rock 8, 9
imperial jade 94
imperial topaz 115
inclusions 87
India 26-27, **46-47**, 86, 149
Indigenous peoples of the
    Americas 88, 96-97, 121,
    130-131
industrial uses 34, 45, 106
intaglios 66
Inuit people 88
ironstone 83
Islam 33, 46, 69

J

jade 18, 80, **92-95**
jadeite 92, 94
Japan, ancient **152-153**
jasper 30, **74-77**, 78-79
jet **134**
jewelery 17, 18, 19, 97
    bracelets 31, 66
    brooches 86, 107, 121
    rings 63, 69, 141
    see also necklaces
jewels **16-17**

K

knives 97, 133
Koroit opal 83

L

labradorite **88-89**
lapis lazuli 31, **90-91**
lasers 45
lava 143
lavender jade 94

lazurite 90
leopard skin jasper 76
lilac jade 94
limestone **145**, 148
lodestone 49
luster 14

M

magnetite 49
mahogany obsidian 143
malachite 51, **52-53**
manganese 68
Mansa Musa 25
Māori people 93, 133
marble 45, **148-149**, 150-151
masks 66, 80, 91, 116, 130-131
    Mesoamerican 50, 53, 96
matrixes 48, 85, 102, 113
Maya civilization 53, 93, 97
medicine 19, 28, 90
melanite 108
memorials 149
Mesoamerican civilizations 50,
    96-97
metamorphic rock 8, 9
Mexican agate 71
Mexican garnet 109
Michelangelo 149
microcrystals 68
minerals 8, **10-13**
    see also gemstones
mirrors 105, 142, 152
Mistress of the Copper Mountain
    53
mixed cuts 17
Mixtec civilization 50
Moche civilization 97
Mohs scale 12-13
Mojave jasper 76
mollusks 120, 121
mookaite 74
moonstone **86**, 87
mosaics 67
moss agate 68
mother-of-pearl 121, **128-131**
mottled jade 94
mottled obsidian 143
Mughal Emerald 103

Mughal Empire 46, 93, 103, 149
Murphy, Jack 41
mussels 120
mutton-fat jade 92

N

nacre 121, 123, 128
    see also mother-of-pearl
Napoleon Bonaparte 35, 43
native elements 9, 11
    copper 32-33, 50, 51, 52, 87
    diamond 13, 34-35, 36-37, 54
    gold 9, 22-25, 26-27
    silver 28-29
nautilus 124
necklaces 60, 67, 69, 91, 103
    shell 121, 132
Neolithic period 75, 93, 143
nephrite 92-95
northern lights 88
nuggets 24, 25, 28

O

obsidian 133, **142-143**
ocean jasper 76
Oceania civilizations **132-133**
Olmec civilization 96, 97
onyx 63, 70
opal **82-85**
orange copper 32
orange diamond 34
orange topaz 115
orange zircon 112
orbicular form 76
ore 24, 28
organic gems 9, 134
    amber 136-137, 138-139
    coral 140-141, 145
    jet 134
    mother-of-pearl 121, 128-131
    peanut wood 135
    pearl 120-123
    shells 18, 124-125, 126-127, 145
oscillation 56
Ostro Stone 115
oxides 11
oysters 120-121

P

padparadscha 40
Palace of Versailles, France 58–59
Pamukkale, Türkiye 145
panning 109
Paraíba tourmaline 98, 100
Parthenon Sculptures 148
peanut wood **135**
pearl **120-123**
   see also mother-of-pearl
pectorals 91, 96, 117
Persian Empire 50, 69
Petra, Jordan 144
phosphates 10
picture jasper 77
"pieces of eight" 29
pineapple opal 85
pink baroque pearls 122
pink opal 84
pink quartz 57
pink ruby 42
pink sapphire 41
pink spinel 49
Pink Star diamond 35
pink topaz 115
pink tourmaline 99
polishing 16
polyps 140
potch opal 84
prasiolite 61
prismatic form 15
pyramidal form 15
pyramids of Giza, Egypt 145
pyrite (fool's gold) 22, 55, 90
pyrope 109

Q

quartz **54-57**, 58–59
   see also agate; amethyst;
     chalcedony

R

rainbow obsidian 143
rarity 14, 17
red amber 136
red beryl 104
red chalcedony 63, 64
red coral 140
red jade 94

red jasper 74
red marble 148
red ruby 42, 45
red zircon 113
refraction 14, 113
religions 18, 41, 43, 103
   Buddhism 46, 47, 153
     Hinduism 44, 46–47, 86, 144
     Islam 33, 46, 69
     see also ancient civilizations
rhodolite 106, 109
rings 63, 69, 141
rock crystal 54
rocks 8–9
   see also sedimentary rock
Rome, ancient 64, **66-67**, 103, 105
royalty *see* crowns
rubellite 99, 100–101
ruby 15, **42-45**
Ruskin, John 98
rutile 57

S

sandstone **144**, 146–147
sapphire **40-41**, 42, 61
sardonyx 63, 65
schrol 99
scientific instruments 33, 45
sea snails 122, 124, 125, 128
seals 69, 75
sedimentary rock 8, 9
   limestone 145
   sandstone 144, 146–147
shale 8
shells 18, **124-125**, 126–127, 145
   see also mother-of-pearl
Sicán civilization 97
Sikhism 27
siliceous sinter 85
Silk Road 91
silver **28-29**
skulls 37, 55
smelting 24
smoky quartz 56
snails 122, 124, 125, 128
South America 96–97
spacecraft 23, 105
spectrolite 89
spessartine 108

spinel **48-49**
sponges 145
Sri Darbār Sāhib, India 26–27
stalactites and stalagmites 52, 53
Star of India sapphire 41
Statue of Liberty, New York 33
status 19, 60, 93, 117
   see also crowns
step cuts 17
sulfates 10
sulfides 11
Sumeria 91
sunstone **87**
swords 19, 35, 117, 152–153
synthetic gems 15

T

Taj Mahal, India 149
temples 26–27, 46–47, 148
Teysky jade 95
thunder eggs 69
tiaras 43
Tiffany, Louis C. 83
tiger's eye 62
titanium andradite 108
Toltec people 129
tools 19, 34, 75, 143
topaz **114-115**
tourmaline 57, **98-101**
trapiche emerald 103
trees 63, 134, 135, 136, 137
tsavorite 106
Tsimshian people 130–131
tumbled jade 94
turban shells 128
turquoise **50**, 80
Tyrian purple 124

U

ultramarine paint 91
uvarovite 106, 108

V

Visigoths 107

W

watches 56
watermelon tourmaline 101
wealth 19, 25

coins 22, 29, 152
weapons 75, 132, 143
   daggers 46, 93
   knives 97, 133
   swords 19, 35, 117, 152–153
West African civilizations 25, 33,
   116-117
Whitby jet 134
white calcite 90
white chalcedony 65
wire gold 25
wire silver 28
wood 63, 134, 135, 136, 137
worms 135

Y

yellow amber 136
yellow amethyst 61
yellow diamond 34
yellow jade 94
yellow jasper 77
yellow topaz 114
yellow tourmaline 99
yellow zircon 112
Yowah opal 82

Z

Zhangye National Geopark, China
   146–147
zircon **112-113**

Acknowledgments

The publisher would like to thank the following people for their assistance in the preparation of this book:
Stefan Podhorodecki for cover Photoshop wizardry; Victoria Pyke for proofreading; Elizabeth Wise for the index; Michelle Crane for editorial help; Anna Pond for design help; Stephen Johnson for image sharpening; and the following for picture research: Samrajkumar S.—Assistant Picture Research Administrator; Nunhoih Guite—Assistant Picture Researcher; Jo Walton—picture researcher

The publisher would like to thank the following for their kind permission to reproduce their photographs:
(Key: a-above; b-below/bottom; c-center; f-far; l-left; r-right; t-top)

1 Dreamstime.com: Afitz. **2-3 Adobe Stock:** Sebastian. **4 Getty Images / iStock:** ScottOrr (br). **6-7 Shutterstock.com:** Albert Russ. **8 Alamy Stock Photo:** Susan E. Degginger (cl). **Dreamstime.com:** Ruslan Minakryn (cb). **Shutterstock.com:** www.sandatlas.org (crb). **8-9 Shutterstock.com:** NatalyFox (Background). **9 Dorling Kindersley:** Natural History Museum, London / Harry Taylor (cb). **Dreamstime.com:** Fireflyphoto (clb). **Getty Images / iStock:** Bestfotostudio (crb). **10 Alamy Stock Photo:** José María Barres Manuel (br). **Dorling Kindersley:** Linda Burgess (cl). **10-11 Adobe Stock:** korkeng. **11 Alamy Stock Photo:** The Natural History Museum (tl). **Dorling Kindersley:** Ruth Jenkinson / Holts Gems (bl); Gary Ombler (bc, br). **Dreamstime.com:** Ruslan Grigolava (tc). **Science Photo Library:** Dirk Wiersma (tr). **12 Dorling Kindersley:** Ruth Jenkinson / Holts Gems (c); Natural History Museum, London / Tim Parmenter (cr). **Science Photo Library:** (cl). **Shutterstock.com:** Elena Grama (bc); SherryArts (bc/Coin); Num Lpphoto (br). **12-13 Adobe Stock:** korkeng (Background). **13 Adobe Stock:** RHJ (cr/Diamond). **Depositphotos Inc:** Bhofack2 (bl); Serkucher (bc). **Dorling Kindersley:** Ruth Jenkinson / Holts Gems (cl/Quartz, cr); Science Museum, London / Dave King (cla); Natural History Museum, London / Tim Parmenter (cra); Natural History Museum, London / Colin Keates (cl, c). **Dreamstime.com:** Bjorn Wylezich (ca). **14 Alamy Stock Photo:** Kerrick James (crb). **Dorling Kindersley:** Natural History Museum, London / Colin Keates (cl). **Dreamstime.com:** Ekaterina Kriminskaia (bl); Mishoo (cla); Halyna Kubei (bc); Mikheewnik (bc/Rarity). **Getty Images / iStock:** E+ / Benedek (clb). **Science Photo Library:** Joel Arem (cb). **Shutterstock.com:** Charoenrit (c). **14-15 Shutterstock.com:** Supa Chan (Background). **15 Dorling Kindersley:** Natural History Museum, London / Colin Keates (cla). **Dreamstime.com:** Lightzoom (bl); Ingemar Magnusson (tr); Aliaksandr Yarmashchuk (cl). **Science Photo Library:** Dirk Wiersma (tc). **Shutterstock.com:** Matteo Chinellato (bc); Albert Russ (c); Diana Elfmarkova (br). **16 Adobe Stock:** Ala (clb); Hawanafsu (crb). **Alamy Stock Photo:** The Natural History Museum (c). **Dreamstime.com:** Bjorn Wylezich (cb). **Shutterstock.com:** Minakryn Ruslan (br). **16-17 Shutterstock.com:** Kogorash (Background). **17 Dorling Kindersley:** Ruth Jenkinson / Holts Gems (c, cr, br); Richard Leeney / Holts Gems, Hatton Garden (cl). **Dreamstime.com:** Vnikitenko (ca). **Shutterstock.com:** Photo33mm (cla/Pink Sapphire); Studio492 (tr). **18 Getty Images:** Corbis Historical / Martha Avery (clb); Dea / De Agostini / G. Dagli Orti (tl). **National Science Foundation, USA:** João Zilhao, University of Bristol (tr). **18-19 Alamy Stock Photo:** Steve Hamblin. **Shutterstock.com:** Hybrid_Graphics (Background). **19 Alamy Stock Photo:** Ilan Amihai (cra); Archive PL (tr); Heritage Image Partnership Ltd (crb); Robert Kawka (cra/Japanese Coin). **Dreamstime.com:** Swisshippo (cra/Medieval Coins); Vitoriaholdingsllc (cra/Chinese Coin); Wirestock (cra/Spanish Coin). **20-21 Shutterstock.com:** Bjoern Wylezich. **22-23 Alamy Stock Photo:** Yuen Man Cheung (bc); CPA Media Pte Ltd / Pictures From History (tc). **Dreamstime.com:** Solaris Images Inc (Background). **22 Adobe Stock:** Ala (bl). **Alamy Stock Photo:** Universal Art Archive (tr). **Los Angeles County Museum of Art:** (ca, cra). **23 Alamy Stock Photo:** Heritage Image Partnership Ltd / © Fine Art Images (br); IanDagnall Computing (cra); World History Archive (clb). **Shutterstock.com:** Photolinc (cra/Frame). **24 Alamy Stock Photo:** Andrey Radchenko (br). **Dreamstime.com:** Gillespaire (tl). **The Metropolitan Museum of Art:** Purchase, 2015 Benefit Fund and Lila Acheson Wallace Gift, 2016 (c). **24-25 Dreamstime.com:** Solaris Images Inc (Background). **25 Alamy Stock Photo:** IanDagnall Computing (br); The Natural History Museum (tr). **Dreamstime.com:** Peter Hermes Furian (tl). **iRocks.com/Rob Lavinsky Photos:** (bl). **Shutterstock.com:** Albert Russ (tc). **26-27 Dreamstime.com:** Xantana. **28 Alamy Stock Photo:** E.R. Degginger (bc). **Dreamstime.com:** Bjrn Wylezich (bl). **Science Photo Library:** Charles D. Winters / Science Photo Library (tl); Joel Arem / Science Photo Library (cl). **28-29 Adobe Stock:** Azahara MarcosDeLeon. **29 Alamy Stock Photo:** Album (tl); The Hoberman Collection (cl). **Bridgeman Images:** Photo © Photo Josse / Bridgeman Images (r). **30 Alamy Stock Photo:** Heritage Image Partnership Ltd / Ashmolean Museum of Art and Archaeology (br); IanDagnall Computing (l). **30-31 Getty Images:** Universal Images Group / Werner Forman (c). **31 Alamy Stock Photo:** Heritage Image Partnership Ltd / © Fine Art Images (bc); Penta Springs Limited / Artokoloro (br). **32 Alamy Stock Photo:** Natural History Museum, London (l, tc). **Dreamstime.com:** Zelenka68 (br). **Getty Images / iStock:** ScottOrr (bc). **32-33 Getty Images / iStock:** Apostrophe. **33 Bridgeman Images:** (c); Photo © Photo Josse / Bridgeman Images (tl); Photo © Dirk Bakker (br). **Dreamstime.com:** Amy Harris (tr). **Powerhouse Collection:** (bl). **34 Alamy Stock Photo:** David J. Green (cla); SBS Eclectic Images (tc); SIPA USA / Sthanlee B. Mirador (br). **Bridgeman Images:** Christie's Images (tr). **Dorling Kindersley:** Ruth Jenkinson / Holts Gems (tc/Yellow). **Fotolia:** Apttone (bl). **34-35 Shutterstock.com:** Sararwut Jaimassiri (Background). **35 Alamy Stock Photo:** Associated Press / Vincent Yu (tl). **Dorling Kindersley:** Ruth Jenkinson / Holts Gems (bl). **Getty Images:** Peter Macdiarmid (cl). **Photo Scala, Florence:** RMN-Grand Palais / Sylvie Chan-Liat / Dist. **Shutterstock.com:** Photolinc (tl/Frame). **36 © DACS 2025:** Damien Hirst. **37 © DACS 2025:** Damien Hirst. **38-39 Shutterstock.com:** Sebastian Janicki. **40 Alamy Stock Photo:** Rhea Eason (bl). **Dorling Kindersley:** Ruth Jenkinson / Holts Gems (cr). **40-41 Dreamstime.com:** Fixzma. **41 Denis Finnin/© AMNH:** (tl). **Bridgeman Images:** Hirmer Fotoarchiv (c). **Dorling Kindersley:** Tim Parmenter / Natural History Museum, London (br). **Dreamstime.com:** Ingemar Magnusson (bl, bc). **Getty Images:** Bettmann (tr). **Shutterstock.com:** photolinc (tr/background). **42 Adobe Stock:** iamtk (br). **Dorling Kindersley:** Ruth Jenkinson / Holts Gems (l). **Shutterstock.com:** photo-world (bc). **42-43 Shutterstock.com:** NatalyFox. **43 Dorling Kindersley:** Tim Parmenter / Natural History Museum, London (cl). **Shutterstock.com:** Kharbine-Tapabor (bc). **The Walters Art Museum, Baltimore:** Acquired by Henry Walters, after 1895 (tr). **44 Alamy Stock Photo:** Pam Biddle (tl); Phil Degginger (b). **44-45 Shutterstock.com:** NatalyFox. **45 Alamy Stock Photo:** Science Photo Library (br). **Science Photo Library:** Natural History Museum, London (tl). **Shutterstock.com:** Albert Russ (tr). **46 Alamy Stock Photo:** Granger—Historical Picture Archive (l). **Courtesy of Salar Jung Museum:** (br). **47 Alamy Stock Photo:** Dinodia Photos (tr); Rafal Cichawa (l). **Bridgeman Images:** Royal Collection Trust / © His Majesty King Charles III, 2025 / Bridgeman Images (br). **48-49 Dreamstime.com:** Mangpor2004. **48 Alamy Stock Photo:** Natural History Museum, London (bc). **Dorling Kindersley:** Tim Parmenter / Natural History Museum, London (tl). **49 Alamy Stock Photo:** View Stock (tc). **Dreamstime.com:** Iamtkb (cl); Ekaterina Kriminskaia (tl, bl). **Getty Images:** Heritage Images / Hulton Archive (cr). **50 Adobe Stock:** Irina (Background). **Alamy Stock Photo:** Phil Degginger (bl); Penta Springs Limited (tr). **The Metropolitan Museum of Art:** Henry G. Leberthon Collection, Gift of Mr. and Mrs. A. Wallace Chauncey, 1957 (br); John Stewart Kennedy Fund, 1915 (tl). **Science Photo Library:** Dirk Wiersma (ca). **50-51 Alamy Stock Photo:** Susan E. Degginger (cr). **51 Alamy Stock Photo:** (cr); Areg Grigoryan (tr). **Science Photo Library:** Joel Arem (bc). **Shutterstock.com:** Apostrophe (Background). **52-53 Shutterstock.com:** Ioluna (Background); Gianni Dagli Orti (tc). **52 Shutterstock.com:** Breck P. Kent (br). **53 Alamy Stock Photo:** Dorling Kindersley ltd (c); Funkyfood London—Paul Williams (br). **Shutterstock.com:** Albert Russ (bl). **54 Alamy Stock Photo:** Pam Biddle (b). **Dreamstime.com:** Silvapinto (tr). **54-55 Getty Images / iStock:** Tevarak (Background). **55 © The Trustees of the British Museum. All rights reserved:** (tr). **Courtesy of the Penn Museum:** (tl). **Science Photo Library:** Millard H. Sharp (bl); Dirk Wiersma (br). **56 Alamy Stock Photo:** Dafinchi (t); Scenics & Science (bc). **Dreamstime.com:** Vvoevale (bl). **Shutterstock.com:** Cagla Acikgoz (br). **56-57 Getty Images / iStock:** Tevarak (Background). **57 Alamy Stock Photo:** imageBROKER.com / Siegra Asmoel (bl); Universal Images Group North America LLC / DeAgostini / R. Appiani (r). **Dreamstime.com:** Bohuslav Jelen (cl); Alfio Scisetti (tl). **58-59 Adobe Stock:** Takashi Images. **60 Dreamstime.com:** Simon Zenger / Simarts (l). **Science Photo Library:** Science Source / Joyce Photographics (tc). **Shutterstock.com:** J. Palys (tr). **60-61 Dorling Kindersley:** Canterbury City Council, Museums and Galleries / Gary Ombler (bc). **Dreamstime.com:** Kateryna Debela (Background). **61 Alamy Stock Photo:** Phil Degginger (br). **Dorling Kindersley:** Ruth Jenkinson / Holts Gems (tc/Polished and Faceted). **Dreamstime.com:** Ekaterina Kriminskaia (tl, tr); Vvoevale (tc). **Trustees of the Natural History Museum, London:** (cr). **Smithsonian Institution:** Chip Clark (cl). **62 Alamy Stock Photo:** Björn Wylezich (l). **62-63 Dreamstime.com:** Ninanaina (Background). **The Metropolitan Museum of Art:** The Jack and Belle Linsky Collection, 1982 (bc). **63 Bridgeman Images:** © A. Dagli Orti / © NPL-DeA Picture Library (tr); Joint Expeditions-Iraq Excavations Fund / Parthian (c). **Christian Mayrhofer/eRocks:** (tl). **Science Photo Library:** Pascal Goetgheluck (bl); Dirk Wiersma (br). **64-65 Dreamstime.com:** Ninanaina (Background). **Science Photo Library:** Natural History Museum, London (c). **64 Dreamstime.com:** Siimsepp (bl). **Shutterstock.com:** Luklinski Grzegorz (tl). **65 Alamy Stock Photo:** CPA Media Pte Ltd / Pictures From History (b); Mike Greenslade (tc). **Depositphotos Inc:** Vvoennyy (tr). **Dreamstime.com:** Bjorn Wylezich (tl). **66 Getty Images:** Dea Picture Library / De Agostini (bl). **The Metropolitan Museum of Art:** Gift of John Taylor Johnston, 1881 (cra). **Shutterstock.com:** Vineyard Perspective (tl). **67 Alamy Stock Photo:** Adam Eastland (crb); History and Art Collection (l). **© The Trustees of the British Museum. All rights reserved:** (tr). **68 Alamy Stock Photo:** The Natural History Museum (bl). **Dorling Kindersley:** Ruth Jenkinson / Holts Gems (tl, cla). **Shutterstock.com:** Albert Russ (tr). **68-69 © The Trustees of the British Museum. All rights reserved:** (tc). **Dorling Kindersley:** Ruth Jenkinson / Holts Gems (bc). **Shutterstock.com:** NatalyFox (Background). **69 Bridgeman Images:** Photo Josse / Persian School (ca). **© The Trustees of the British Museum. All rights reserved:** (cla, cr). **Shutterstock.com:** Albert Russ (cra). **70 Alamy Stock Photo:** Thomas Cockrem (tr). **Dorling Kindersley:** Natural History Museum, London / Tim Parmenter (tc). **Dreamstime.com:** Afitz (tl). **70-71 Science Photo Library:** Millard H. Sharp (b). **Shutterstock.com:** NatalyFox (Background). **71 Alamy Stock Photo:** DPA Picture Alliance (br); The Natural History Museum (tr). **72-73 Shutterstock.com:** Sebastian Janicki. **74 Dorling Kindersley:** Natural History Museum, London / Tim Parmenter (cra). **Dreamstime.com:** Ekaterina Kriminskaia (tr); Bjorn Wylezich (ca); Mrreporter (b). **74-75 Dreamstime.com:** Cougarsan (Background). **75 Alamy Stock Photo:** Biosphoto / Pascal Goetgheluck (cr). **© The Trustees of the British Museum. All rights reserved:** (bc). **The Metropolitan Museum of Art:** Purchase, Edward S. Harkness Gift, 1926 (c). **The Walters Art Museum, Baltimore:** Acquired by Henry Walters, 1900 (t). **76 Alamy Stock Photo:** SuperStock / RGB Ventures / Fred Hirschmann (c, bl). **Dreamstime.com:** Yury Kosourov (tl); Photowitch (tr); Underwatermaui (bc). **Getty Images / iStock:** Estellez (br). **76-77 Dreamstime.com:** Cougarsan (Background). **77 Alamy Stock Photo:** Ron Evans (cla). **Dreamstime.com:** Miriam Doerr (bl). **Science Photo Library:** Dirk Wiersma (tl). **Shutterstock.com:** Olpo (r). **78-79 Science Photo Library:** Dirk Wiersma. **80 Alamy Stock Photo:** Pictures Now (tl). **Bridgeman Images:** Bronze Age (crb). **Dorling Kindersley:** University of Pennsylvania Museum of Archaeology and Anthropology / Angela Coppola (bc). **80-81 The Metropolitan Museum of Art:** Gift of Florence and Herbert Irving, 2015 (tc). **81 Getty Images:** Corbis Historical / Asian Art & Archaeology, Inc. / Martha Avery. **82 Alamy Stock Photo:** Zoonar / Heinz Meis (l). **Shutterstock.com:** Finesell (br); Abdul Matloob (bc). **82-83 Shutterstock.com:** Marina Yesina (Bacground). **83 Alamy Stock Photo:** Album (tl); Blickwinkel / C-Goemi (bl). **Courtesy Altmann + Cherny:** (tr). **Dorling Kindersley:** Natural History Museum, London / Colin Keates (br). **Dreamstime.com:** Vvoevale (bc/2). **Getty Images / iStock:** Oksana Tabachenkova (bc). **84-85 Shutterstock.com:** Marina Yesina (Background). **84 Dorling Kindersley:** Natural History Museum, London / Colin Keates (tl). **85 Australian Opal Centre:** Robert A. Smith (fbr). **Dorling Kindersley:** Natural History Museum, London / Colin Keates (cra). **Mathew Carey, Kings Opals:** (fcr). **Photo courtesy of James St. John (Ohio State University at Newark):** (tr). **Shutterstock.com:** Albert Russ (cb). **86 Alamy Stock Photo:** Valery Voennyy (br). **Dorling Kindersley:** Ruth Jenkinson / Holts Gems (bc, bc/Unusual colour); Natural History Museum, London / Colin Keates (tl). **Getty Images / iStock:** Svetolk (Background). **The Metropolitan Museum of Art:** Gift of Mr. and Mrs. Uzi Zucker, 1981 (cl). **Photo Scala, Florence:** Image copyright The Metropolitan Museum of Art / Art Resource (tr). **87 Dorling Kindersley:** Ruth Jenkinson / Holts Gems (br); Natural History Museum, London / Colin Keates (tc). **Dreamstime.com:** Iamtkb (tc/Inner Glow). **Getty Images / iStock:** Reimphoto (tl). **National Museum of Natural History / Smithsonian Institution:** (bl/1, br/1). **Science Photo Library:** Vaughan Fleming (bl). **Shutterstock.com:** White Snow (Background). **88-89 Adobe Stock:** Sebastian (c). **Dreamstime.com:** Dawn Hudson (Background). **88 Dorling Kindersley:** Colin Keates / Natural History Museum, London (tr). **Getty Images:** Noppawat Tom Charoensinphon (bl). **89 Adobe Stock:** Henri Koskinen (br). **Science Photo Library:** DK Images / Science Photo Library (tl); Vaughan Fleming / Science Photo Library (tr). **90 Dreamstime.com:** Nika Lerman (tl); Alexander Nedviga (cla); Mrreporter (cl, bl); Lori Martin (clb). **Shutterstock.com:** Sebastian Janicki (br). **90-91 The Metropolitan Museum of Art:** Dodge Fund, 1933 (bc). **Shutterstock.com:** Addictive Creative (Background). **91 Alamy Stock Photo:** World History Archive (cb). **Dreamstime.com:** Michal Janoek / Wesleyc1701 (r). **Getty Images:** Universal Images Group / Universal History Archive (tl). **Shutterstock.com:** Prokrida (tl/Frame). **92 Adobe Stock:** NOKFreelance (Background). **Alamy Stock Photo:** ZUMA Press, Inc. (bl). **Dreamstime.com:** Vvoevale (tr). **Getty Images:** Bloomberg (crb). **Sothebys London, December 4, 10:37 PM IST, Lot 7; New York Private Collection, acquired before 1964; © Photo courtesy Sothebys, 2024.**. **Science Photo Library:** Phil Degginger (tc); Dirk Wiersma (tl). **Shutterstock.com:** photolinc (crb/ Frame). **93 Alamy Stock Photo:** Sipa US / Imaginechina / Pu Feng (tl); ZUMA Press, Inc. / SIPA Asia (b). **Bridgeman Images:** Maori (crb). **The Metropolitan Museum of Art:** Bequest of George C. Stone, 1935 (tr). **94 Alamy Stock Photo:** Valery Voennyy (c); YongXin Zhang (br). **Dorling Kindersley:** Natural History Museum, London / Tim Parmenter (bl). **Dreamstime.com:** Chernetskaya (cr); Vvoevale (tl); Kongsky (cr/Rock). **Getty Images / iStock:** VvoeVale (tc). **94-95 Adobe Stock:** NOKFreelance (Background). **95 Alamy Stock Photo:** CPA Media Pte Ltd / Pictures From History (clb); Valery Voennyy (tl). **Dorling Kindersley:** Durham University Oriental Museum / Gary Ombler (r). **96-97 Alamy Stock Photo:** Album (tc). **96 Alamy Stock Photo:** Album (r); Heritage Image Partnership Ltd (tl). **The Metropolitan Museum of Art:** Bequest of Alice K. Bache, 1977 (bl). **97 Getty Images:** DEA / G. Dagli Orti (r). **98 Adobe Stock:** Sebastian (l). **Alamy Stock Photo:** Greg C Grace (br). **Dreamstime.com:** Micropic (bc). **99 Adobe Stock:** dcw25 (tr). **Alamy Stock Photo:** Heritage Image Partnership Ltd / Ashmolean Museum of Art and Archaeology (cr); Tibbut Archive (tr/artwork). **Dreamstime.com:** Micropic (br); Ruslan Minakryn (bl). **The Metropolitan Museum of Art:** Bequest of Edmund C. Converse, 1921 (tl). **Shutterstock.com:** Azka Photographer Pro (bc); Albert Russ (bc/Schrol). **100 Brian Cook:** (bl). **Dreamstime.com:** Miriam Doerr (tc); Mrreporter (br). **Shutterstock.com:** photolinc. **100-101 Shutterstock.com:** Kogorash. **101 Alamy Stock Photo:** blickwinkel (bl). **Depositphotos Inc:** Minakryn. **Science Photo Library:** Dirk Wiersma (tl). **102 Alamy Stock Photo:** John Cancalosi (br). **Dorling Kindersley:** Ruth Jenkinson / Holts Gems (bc). **Dreamstime.com:** Digitalpress (bc/Rough). **Getty Images / iStock:** photo-world (l). **102-103 Dreamstime.com:** Flas100. **103 Bridgeman Images:** Christie's Images / Bridgeman Images (ftr, br). **© The Trustees of the British Museum. All rights reserved:** (bc). **Getty Images:** Guillermo Legaria / Stringer (bl). **The Metropolitan Museum of Art:** Purchase, Lila Acheson Wallace Gift, Acquisitions Fund and Mary Trumbull Adams Fund, 2015 (cl). **104-105 Dreamstime.com:** Flas100 (Background). **104 Alamy Stock Photo:** Corbin17 (bc). **Dorling Kindersley:** Ruth Jenkinson / Holts Gems (tl). **Dreamstime.com:** Micropic (bl). **Shutterstock.com:** Breck P. Kent (tr). **105 Dorling Kindersley:** Ruth Jenkinson / Holts Gems (bl). **Dreamstime.com:** Nemes Laszlo (tr). **Getty Images:** Brendan Smialowski / AFP (bc). **The Metropolitan Museum of Art:** Fletcher Fund, 1925 (tl). **Science Photo Library:** Roberto De Gugliemo (br). **Shutterstock.com:** Albert Russ (bc/ Heliodor). **106 Adobe Stock:** Mblindia (bc). **Dreamstime.com:** Ruslan Minakryn (tr). **106-107 Shutterstock.com:** Ratana21 (Background). **107 Alamy Stock Photo:** Maidun Collection (cra); SBS Eclectic Images (tc). **Bridgeman Images:** National Museums Liverpool (br). **The Cleveland Museum Of Art:** Purchase from the J. H. Wade Fund (tl). **The Walters Art Museum, Baltimore:** Acquired by Henry Walters, 1930 (clb). **108-109 Shutterstock.com:** Ratana21 (Background). **108 Dreamstime.com:** Ekaterina Kriminskaia (br); Vvoevale (t). **Shutterstock.com:** Lewalp (bl); Albert Russ (bc). **109 Alamy Stock Photo:** Phil Degginger (tl); William Mullins (cra). **Dreamstime.com:** Mrreporter (b); Vvoevale (tc). **110-111 Bridgeman Images:** Birmingham Museums Trust / Bridgeman Images. **112 Alamy Stock Photo:** Ron Evans (tl). **Dorling Kindersley:** Natural History Museum, London / Colin Keates (cb). **John Valley, University of Wisconsin-Madison:** (bl). **Science Photo Library:** Joel Arem (br/X2). **113 Alamy Stock Photo:** Derek Anderson (tl). **Dreamstime.com:** Igor Kaliuzhnyi (tr); Bjorn Wylezich (c). **Science Photo Library:** Joel Arem (b/X3). **114-115 Dreamstime.com:** Dawn Hudson. **114 Getty Images / iStock:** rep0rter (bl). **115 Alamy Stock Photo:** Digital Image Library (cla). **Dorling Kindersley:** Colin Keates / Natural History Museum, London (tl, c); Ruth Jenkinson / Holts Gems (r). **Dreamstime.com:** Enguerrandcales (cl). **Science Photo Library:** Roberto De Guliemo / Science Photo Library (br). **116 The Metropolitan Museum of Art:** Edith Perry Chapman Fund, 1975 (br); The Michael C. Rockefeller Memorial Collection, Purchase, Nelson A. Rockefeller Gift, 1967 (l). **116-117 Alamy Stock Photo:** Peter Horree (c). **117-118 © The Trustees of the British Museum. All rights reserved:** (t). **117 Photo Scala, Florence:** The Metropolitan Museum of Art / Art Resource (bc). **120 Dreamstime.com:** Subbotina (t). **120-121 Dreamstime.com:** Amandee (Background). **Getty Images:** Hulton Fine Art Collection / Culture Club (bc). **Newfields:** (tc). **121 Courtesy of Indianapolis Museum of Art at Newfields.:** Gift of Mr. Earl C. Townsend, Jr., 61.88. (tl). **The Metropolitan Museum of Art:** Purchase, Susan and Jon Rotenstreich Gift, 2001 (tr). **122 Adobe Stock:** Elena (cra). **Alamy Stock Photo:** Yuri Arcurs (tl); William Scott (tr). **Dorling Kindersley:** Richard Leeney / Holts Gems, Hatton Garden (br). **Dreamstime.com:** Cammeraydave (c). **Giga Pearl, Photo by Johann Bona:** (bl). **Shutterstock.com:** photolinc (c/Frame). **122-123 Dreamstime.com:** Amandee (Background). **123 Alamy Stock Photo:** BFA (br). **Dorling Kindersley:** Ruth Jenkinson / Holts Gems (bl); Natural History Museum, London / Colin Keates (tl). **Getty Images / iStock:** Karayuschij (tr). **Shutterstock.com:** photolinc (br/Frame). **124-125 Alamy Stock Photo:** Interfoto / Zoology (c). **Shutterstock.com:** Hybrid_Graphics. **124 Dreamstime.com:** Ekays (br). **Getty Images / iStock:** Joingate (bl); jon841 (cl). **Shutterstock.com:** SKT Studio (cla). **125 The Cleveland Museum Of Art:** Gift of Homer H. Tielke Jr., in honor of the fortieth wedding anniversary of Mr. and Mrs. Homer H. Tielke Sr. (cr). **Getty Images:** Paul Starosta (br). **The Metropolitan Museum of Art:** The Crosby Brown Collection of Musical Instruments, 1889 (bl). **Shutterstock.com:** Aakruti (ftr). **126-127 Shutterstock.com:** olpo. **128 Dorling Kindersley:** (cl); Ruth Jenkinson / Holts Gems (tl). **128-129 Shutterstock.com:** Marina Yesina. **129 Dorling Kindersley:** Michel Zabe / CONACULTA-INAH-MEX / Michel Zabé. **130 The Metropolitan Museum of Art:** The Charles and Valerie Diker Collection of Native American Art, Gift of Charles and Valerie Diker, 2019. **131 Alamy Stock Photo:** Penta Springs / Penta Springs Limited. **132 The Metropolitan Museum of Art:** The Michael C. Rockefeller Memorial Collection, Gift of Nelson A. Rockefeller, 1972 (l). **Aunty Corrie Fullard, much respected palawa elder of the Tasmanian Aboriginal community, 1931–2023:** (tc). **132-133 © The Trustees of the British Museum. All rights reserved:** (c). **133 akg-images:** Interfoto / Hermann Historica GmbH (tr). **© The Trustees of the British Museum. All rights reserved:** (l). **Getty Images:** Universal Images Group / Werner Forman (br). **134 Alamy Stock Photo:** Alan Curtis (tl); RTM / Piemags (cra, cra/ Dice). **Dorling Kindersley:** Ruth Jenkinson / Holts Gems (tc); Natural History Museum, London / Tim Parmenter (cl, bl). **Dreamstime.com:** Vvoevale (cla). **Shutterstock.com:** Melodist (Background). **134-135 © The Trustees of the British Museum. All rights reserved:** (bc). **135 Alamy Stock Photo:** Ron Evans (bl). **Crystal World Exhibition Centre:** (tl). **Shutterstock.com:** Luria (Background). **Roland Smithies and Sarah Smithies:** (fbr, br). **136 Adobe Stock:** IGOR (tl). **Dreamstime.com:** Roksolana Mykytiv (bc); Igor Stramyk (br). **Science Photo Library:** Pascal Goetgheluck (bl). **136-137 Dreamstime.com:** Suthisa Kaewkajang; Suthisa Kaewkajang. **Dreamstime.com:** Suthisa Kaewkajang; Suthisa Kaewkajang. **136-137 Dreamstime.com:** Suthisa Kaewkajang; Suthisa Kaewkajang. **Dreamstime.com:** Suthisa Kaewkajang; Suthisa Kaewkajang. **137 Alamy Stock Photo:** PjrStudio (tr). **Getty Images / iStock:** Nada Bascarevic (br). **Royal Saskatchewan Museum (RSM/ R.C. McKellar:** (tl). **The Metropolitan Museum of Art:** Bequest of Edmund C. Converse, 1921 (bl); Gift of Gustavus A. Pfeiffer, 1948 (cr). **Shutterstock.com:** photolinc (br/ background). **138-139 Getty Images:** Thomas Imo / Photothek. **140-141 Shutterstock.com:** TairA. **140 Alamy Stock Photo:** Ron Evans (br); The Print Collector / Heritage Images (tr). **Dreamstime.com:** Foto21293 (bl). **Shutterstock.com:** photolinc (tr/Frame). **141 Bridgeman Images:** Ashmolean Museum (br). **Dorling Kindersley:** Gary Ombler / Durham University Oriental Museum (l); Ruth Jenkinson / Holts Gems (cr). **Dreamstime.com:** Hapelena (cl); Vvoevale (tc); Imma Gambardella (tr). **142 Alamy Stock Photo:** geoz (cb); Triangle Travels (cla). **© The Trustees of the British Museum. All rights reserved:** (tl). **143 Adobe Stock:** Björn Wylezich (bc). **Bridgeman Images:** Christie's Images (cl). **Dorling Kindersley:** Ruth Jenkinson / Holts Gems (tc); Oxford University Museum of Natural History / Gary Ombler (bc/Conchoidal fracture). **Dreamstime.com:** Enguerrandcales (br). **Getty Images:** Corbis Documentary / Layne Kennedy (crb). **National Museum of Natural History / Smithsonian Institution:** (fbl, tr/1, fcr, fcrb). **Shutterstock.com:** Dima Moroz (tr). **144 Adobe Stock:** Maribor (Background); SergioDenisenko (cra). **Dorling Kindersley:** Ruth Jenkinson / Holts Gems (bl). **The Metropolitan Museum of Art:** (br). **Shutterstock.com:** photolinc (cra/ Frame). **145 Alamy Stock Photo:** Classic Image (clb); LGPL / Alan Curtis (br). **Depositphotos Inc:** Shebeko (Background). **Dreamstime.com:** Martina Badini (bc). **146-147 Adobe Stock:** Thongchai S. **148 Adobe Stock:** Rixie (bl). **Dreamstime.com:** Matteo Galimberti (ftl). **Gerald Lucy:** (tc). **148-149 Dreamstime.com:** Nastya81 (c). **Shutterstock.com:** Venture Stone Creator (background). **149 Los Angeles County Museum of Art:** The Phil Berg Collection / Umar ibn Ali (bc). **Shutterstock.com:** gurb101088 (r); Jumo32 (tl). **150-151 Getty Images / iStock:** tunart. **152-153 Tokyo National Museum/DNP Art Communications:** (tc). **Shutterstock.com:** Eleni Mavrandoni (c). **152 Alamy Stock Photo:** Hoberman Publishing / The Hoberman Collection (bl). **153 Tokyo National Museum/ DNP Art Communications:** (c). **The Metropolitan Museum of Art:** Rogers Fund, 1904 (cr). **154-160 Shutterstock.com:** Joann Vector Artist (background)

Cover images: *Front and Back:* **Shutterstock.com:** detchana wangkheeree (golden layer), korkeng (blue layer), Tommy Lauren; *Front:* **Dorling Kindersley:** Gary Ombler / Holts Gems ftr, Tim Parmenter / Natural History Museum, London tr, ftr/ (Topaz); **Dreamstime.com:** Ijp2726 bl; **Shutterstock.com:** Michael Benjamin (texture); *Back:* **Alamy Stock Photo:** PjrStudio ftr, Tetra Images cr, The Natural History Museum bl; **Dorling Kindersley:** Natural History Museum, London / Colin Keates tl; **Dreamstime.com:** Afitz bc, Vvoevale tr; **Science Photo Library:** Millard H. Sharp br; **Shutterstock.com:** korkeng (background), Abdul Matloob tc; *Spine:* **Dreamstime.com:** Ruslan Minakryn t; **Shutterstock.com:** detchana wangkheeree (gold texture)

Endpaper image: Shutterstock.com: Albert Russ.